The

B B C

Black Bean Counter

Demystifying the Accounting Profession

Praise for *The Black Bean Counter*

*'This is an interesting and practical book. I love
how you developed your story and kept me
glued (and I believe same for any reader as well)
throughout the book. Quite a page-turner you
have here. Great work'.*

Jessie Raymond, book editor.

The
B B C
Black Bean Counter

Demystifying the Accounting Profession

LANCE KADIRI

Disclaimer

It is hereby acknowledged that the information used in the book has come from a variety of sources. No attempt has been made to misuse information but only to enlighten the audience. Every attempt has also been made to avoid the infringement of any copyright. Any perceived infringement is therefore unintended and regretted. The use of any of the contents of the book other than for educational purposes requires express permission of the publishers.

Published in the United Kingdom in 2023 by Framichi publications.

www.framichipublications.com

DEDICATION

I dedicate this book to my beloved father, Capt. Sheriff Kadiri, for believing in my abilities and for the love and guidance.

You are the best dad in the world.

ACKNOWLEDGEMENT

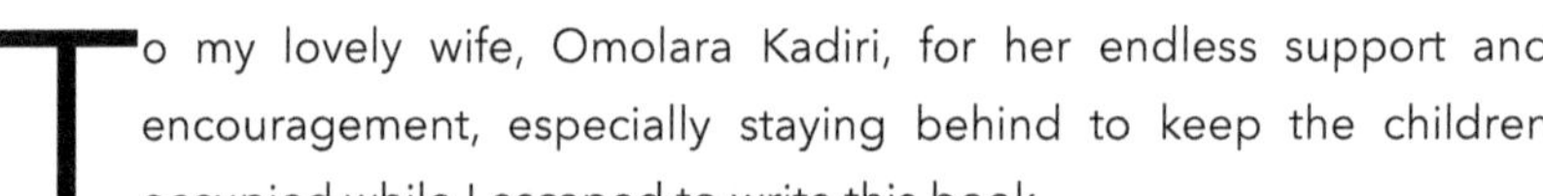

To my lovely wife, Omolara Kadiri, for her endless support and encouragement, especially staying behind to keep the children occupied while I escaped to write this book.

To all the partners and managers at the accounting firms I worked and trained at, who all showed me the ropes. Also, to my former partners at Lance Lincoln and Lance Taggart West, for believing in the vision of the partnership.

To the staff of Jollof Zone in Edgware for their hospitality and fantastic customer service on the days I visited the restaurant for my regular sessions with my book-writing consultant.

To the staff of Spearmans Consulting for their assistance during the book writing process.

A big thank you to my book writing consultant, Franca B Lawrence, for her professionalism, guidance, and immense knowledge about the book writing process, without which this book could not have been written.

Lastly, I thank my publisher, Framichi Publications, for being the one-stop shop for all my publication needs. They made the publishing process seamless by taking care of everything on my behalf.

TABLE OF CONTENTS

Dedication v

Acknowledgement vi

Chapter One Background To My Story 1

Chapter Two Coming To The United Kingdom 6

Chapter Three Coming To The United Kingdom 16

Chapter Four Meeting My Mother For The First Time 28

Chapter Five My University Years 36

Chapter Six Route To Qualification 44

Chapter Seven The Life Of A Trainee Accountant 54

Chapter Eight The Professional Struggle Begins 69

Chapter Nine Starting My Own Firm 82

Chapter Ten A New Chapter In My Life 93

Chapter Eleven The Birth Of My Spearmans Business Empire 107

Chapter Twelve My Message To The Next Generation 119

About The Black Bean Counter 127

Chapter One

Background To My Story

A SURVEY CONDUCTED by the group Business in the Community in 2019 and published by the Guardian news website on 22 June 2020 revealed that only 1.5% of black professionals in the UK hold leadership positions out of the 3.7m leadership positions across the UK. For ethnic minorities in general, the statistics are a total of 10.4% compared to 89.6% of white professionals in leadership positions. (Source: www. theguardian.com)

These shocking statistics came as no surprise to me. I am Lance Kadiri, popularly known as the Black Bean Counter (BBC). As a black professional in the UK and an accountant with over thirty-five years of experience in the industry, I have lived through the challenges of breaking that proverbial glass ceiling because the pinnacle of every accountant's career is to become the finance director of a large company. Yet very few of us can achieve that.

To put this into perspective, I know of only one black accountant who made it into that tiny 1.5% bracket to become the finance director of a large international company. Shocking, isn't it? So how does one accomplish this feat? That is why I have written this book. I want the next generation of young black and other ethnic minority professionals to have a better experience than my generation did. This book will offer tips on how you can break that glass ceiling.

In addition, you will learn how to have a successful career as a black professional in the United Kingdom, whether you break that glass ceiling or not. Nothing should deter you from achieving success. What better way to shine the light for the youths than sharing my journey and experience in a book that would help them to navigate the pitfalls and challenges of succeeding as a black professional in the UK.

My story is a remarkable one because a career in accountancy was not my dream until my dear father steered me in that direction. I was a teenager growing up in Lagos, Nigeria, with consistently bad grades in mathematics. I was at the top of my class with very good grades in other subjects except Mathematics. There is a myth that you must be a mathematical genius to qualify as an accountant. So how did I become an accountant with such poor grades in Mathematics? Good question! Keep reading to find out my route to qualification. I am proof that you do not have to be a mathematical genius to become an accountant, and I hope my story will inspire anyone out there with such career aspirations.

My migration to the United Kingdom at the age of eighteen was a revelation. It changed everything. Keep reading to discover how a teenage African immigrant overcame the challenges of integrating into a foreign western country, from achieving my GCSEs in mathematics to graduation from university and the difficult training to become a qualified accountant in Liverpool city.

After many years working for large, non-ethnic minority international accounting firms with mostly black sports and entertainment stars for clients, I observed that these white-owned firms did not understand the cultural aspect of the spending patterns of black people. I saw many black clients mismanage their hard-earned money and ended up penniless. It takes a black person to fully understand the context of our attitude to money. I knew I could be a better accountant to that market segment by providing bespoke advice to them instead of the ineffective one-size-fits-all approach.

I spotted a niche in the market, grabbed the opportunity, and my accounting firm, Spearmans Consulting, was born. A second goal for setting up my own firm was a desire to help black business owners with the 'tools' to run their businesses more professionally. After twenty-two years, I can confirm that I have succeeded in helping a vast number of businesses from every industry and sector, not just black-owned businesses. This book will reveal how I accomplished that.

This is my legacy; documented nuggets of valuable life lessons that will be passed from generation to generation. This book is for anyone who dreams of becoming a successful professional in the UK, but especially for immigrants searching for answers and guidance not found in government books.

In conclusion, my book advocates for parents to take a more active role in their children's education and career, as my father did with mine. There is a school of thought that parents should not interfere in a child's career and that children should be permitted to decide their career choices. My story will reveal that parents get it right sometimes. Based on that premise, I believe parents should continue to provide that much-needed guidance.

That is why this book is somewhat a long 'thank you letter' to my father, Capt. Sheriff Kadiri, for believing in my abilities and for the love and guidance.

The readers will learn immensely from my journey through life and how I navigated various aspects of it. I am certain they will be entertained too. Enjoy the book.

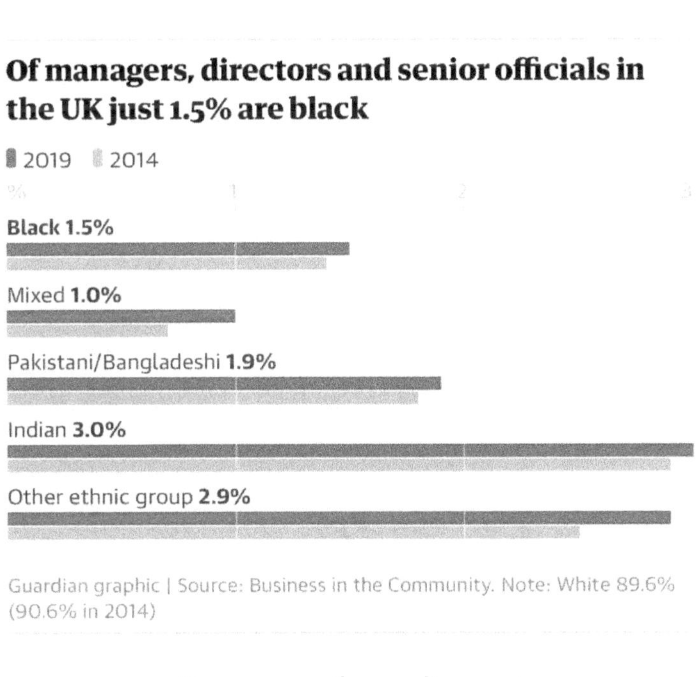

(Source: www.theguardian.com)

Chapter Two
Coming To The United Kingdom

I COULD BE described as someone who has led a 'charmed' life because of my childhood experience. I base this on the fact that I was unusually affected by the difficulties of being raised by people who are not my parents. There are countless stories of mistreatment and child abuse when a child is left in such situations, but mine was the opposite. I was definitely one of the lucky ones.

I was born in Lagos, Nigeria, in the central business district (CDB) of Itafaji, a famous Lagos market. Itafaji is located on Lagos Island, one of the biggest commercial centres in Lagos City. Itafaji is also popularly known as the town that never sleeps.

GROWING UP WITHOUT MY PARENTS

My parents moved to the United Kingdom in 1962, shortly after I was born, and I was left behind in Nigeria to be raised by my maternal grandmother and aunt. I do not know why my parents did not take me with them then, but knowing what I know now about my loving parents, they must have had good reasons for that decision. Besides, it was a widespread practice in Nigeria to leave young kids to be raised by their grandparents. It was usually to enable the parents to focus on attaining some financial stability before bringing the kids to live with them. My parents were no different. They had to settle down in the UK, a country that is well known for exorbitant childcare costs.

My grandmother's house was located on Willoughby Street, which was named after my grandmother's family because they were the first settlers on that road. I lived with my grandmother and aunt in Itafaji from 1961 to 1969, which was a period of eight years. I loved living with my grandmother because she pampered and doted on me as grandparents often do. My fondest memory was when she bought me a suit and lace-up shoes and asked me to do a catwalk like a model in front of her. I could see the joy and laughter it brought her. However, she ensured I did my chores and learned to take responsibility for tidying up and helping around the house as much as possible. This was a great foundation for me because I grew up to be hard-working and responsible early in my life.

Grandma also made sure I studied hard and took my schoolwork very seriously. I attended Holy Cross primary school on Lagos Island and was always amongst the top five in the class, which made my grandmother and aunt immensely proud. My parents were thankful for this too. The values my grandmother taught me stayed with me all my life, and I remain grateful for them.

My parents' marriage ended when I was eight years old, and my father decided I should not live with my maternal grandmother anymore, but because I loved my grandmother and was happy living there, they decided the best thing to do was to trick me into leaving my grandmother's house. The trick was to make me believe I was going to the UK to join my parents. The first part of the plan was to throw a big send-off party for me. I had so much fun and received lots of presents. All my neighbours came to the send-off party to bid me farewell before my supposed departure to the UK. The second part of the plan was to be taken away by my father's friend, Alhaji B A Savage, with the pretext that I was being taken to the airport to board the flight to the UK. I was excited about that and happily jumped on the ferry to embark on my journey. That was the last time I saw my grandmother because she died six years later.

To my greatest surprise, Alhaji Savage took me to his home on Ademuyiwa Street, Off Apapa Road in Ebute-Meta. Alhaji Savage was my father's close friend and colleague because he was a commercial manager of a shipping line.

The realisation that I was not going to the UK, after all, was unbearable to my young mind, and the next morning, I ran away to my uncle's house, which was one mile away. I arrived there with tears streaming down my face. I cried that I did not want to live with Alhaji Savage and his family, whom I barely knew. They were strangers to me. My young mind could not comprehend why I was taken away from my beloved grandmother to live with strangers. I was also upset that I was not going to the UK as promised. I asked my uncle if I could stay with him, and he said no because my father wanted me to live with Alhaji Savage and his family. I calmed down after a while, and my uncle brought me back to Alhaji Savage, who was very understanding and kind to me. I ran away three more times within my first week at that house before I finally settled down and accepted my fate that this was going to be my new home for now. When I did, I began to enjoy my stay with Alhaji Savage.

The family treated me like a special guest, and to the kids, I was just one of them, which made it even easier for me to fit in. Mrs Savage treated me like one of her kids, and there was no special treatment. The Savages were very nice people, and we lived together as one big happy family. The house was in a big compound with several houses, which meant many families and children, and we all went to the same school, St Paul's primary school.

Whenever I came home with good grades on my school report card, Alhaji Savage took me to Kingsway shopping mall and bought me anything I wanted as a treat. This was the second time in my childhood that I was raised by people who were not my parents, and once again, I had a happy experience. Not once did I miss my parents because I was never treated badly. If I had been maltreated, I probably would have longed for them every day, so I am glad I did not experience that.

There was a similarity in the environment in which I was raised. Although I lived with my grandmother on Lagos Island and with Alhaji Savage on the Mainland, which were opposite locations in Lagos, one thing was the same. Both streets I grew up on were vibrant commercial centres. Ademuyiwa Street in Ebute Meta was also a bustling commercial centre that attracted market traders from all over Nigeria.

Looking back, I cannot help wondering if this unique environment of my childhood influenced my love for commerce and why I ended up as an accountant and business consultant, helping businesses to thrive. It may also explain my entrepreneurial spirit and why I own businesses of my own. Something else worthy of note is that my parents are Muslims, but I was sent to Christian schools both on the island and mainland, which showed my parents' broad-minded approach to my education.

I lived with Alhaji Savage and his family for two years until age ten. After my parents divorced, my mother remained in the United Kingdom. My father remarried and had two daughters with my stepmother.

When I was ten years old, my father returned to Nigeria with his wife and daughters, and they settled in Apapa GRA. I was finally able to live with a parent for the first time in my life. My 'charmed' life continued, and I was once again treated specially by my stepmother.

It was great to have siblings, and my two half-sisters were lovely, and we got on very well. I took the lead as the big brother to help with the chores. I was treated with much love by the whole family, and based on that, I can gladly confirm that I have no wicked stepmother tales to share.

SECONDARY SCHOOL YEARS

The time soon came for me to go to secondary school, and I was sent to boarding school at Ijebu Divisional Multilateral Grammar School in the village of Ijebu. It was a shock to go from living in an urban city like Lagos to living in a rural area like Ijebu. I soon adapted to my new surroundings and began to enjoy boarding school. I made many friends and had a happy time at school. I was there for six years. I was a clever kid and had good grades. I would score 98% in economics and most of my subjects but could not pass mathematics.

I missed my family, but I could only come home for the two weeks of Easter break in April and the six weeks of summer holiday in June. My father visited once a year, but my uncle, who lived near the Ijebu village, visited me more frequently. My paternal grandmother's cousin lived in the village, and I visited them at weekends to enjoy a much-needed home-cooked meal because, as we all know, school meals were not good enough.

In 1967, my dad was promoted to the position of the Managing Director of a subsidiary of the UK arm of a shipping line. (I must point out that my dad was the first Nigerian to captain an ocean-going ship. Prior to his promotion to the position of ship captain, the ships were captained by Caucasians).

The promotion to managing director necessitated my dad's relocation back to the UK. Before he left, he showed me my Nigerian international passport to assure me that I would join him and the rest of the family someday. However, he never said when that day would be. That year, 1976, was two years before I completed secondary school.

With my family back in the UK, I could no longer go home to Apapa GRA for my holidays. Instead, I was once more sent to live with another friend of my dad's named Mr R A Deen. For the next two years, I stayed with the Deens in Iganmu, a fast-developing mainland area. This was also the famous FESTAC 77 period when Iganmu was the main location for the festival. ("*FESTAC 77, also known as the **Second World Black and African Festival of Arts and Culture,** was a major international festival held in Lagos, Nigeria, from 15 January 1977 to 12 February 1977. The hosting of the festival led to the establishment of the Nigerian National Council of Arts and Culture, Festac Village and the National Theatre, Iganmu, Lagos*").

(Source: www.en.wikipedia.com)

Mr Deen, or Uncle Deen as he was known to us, was the only son of a wealthy merchant lady, and he drove a Range Rover. To drive such a luxury car at that time shows just how wealthy Uncle Deen was. He built two brand new twin bungalows in Iganmu, and I even had a room to myself. Mr Deen had a big family because he had three wives and many children. All the wives and children loved me, and all I have are happy memories of living with the Deens.

In June 1978, I wrote my WAEC exams, and my dad did not wait for my result to be released because it would take a few months before that happened. Therefore, my dad returned to Nigeria in July to take me on that long-awaited journey to the UK. We left Nigeria on 31st July and arrived in the UK on 1st August 1978.

We arrived at Manchester Airport and took a black cab to Liverpool. It was a thirty-minute journey. On arrival in the UK, the imagery that stuck with me was the amazing green colour of the grass compared to the dull sunburnt colour of the Tropical Nigerian grass. I also remember the size of the cows I saw grazing in the countryside as we drove past in the black cab. The cows were big and healthy, unlike the skinny cows I often saw in Nigeria.

We arrived at our home in Heswall, a town on the Wirral, Merseyside, about 6.3 miles from Liverpool, England. I was sixteen years old when I arrived in the UK, just two months before my seventeenth birthday. I was excited to be back with my family again, and at that moment, I knew that my days of living with relatives and friends of my father were finally behind me. I was a teenager in an exciting new country and could not wait for the adventure to begin.

My dad's certificate of qualification as a ship captain. The first Nigerian to achieve this qualification.

A photo of my dad in the sixties.

Chapter Three
Coming To The United Kingdom

NYONE WHO MIGRATED to a foreign country would understand the importance of integrating into that society. This refers to social, cultural, and economic integration.

The Cambridge Dictionary defines integration as follows:

"To mix with and join society or a group of people, often changing to suit their way of life, habits, and customs."

(www.dictionary.Cambridge.org)

Research has shown that immigrant children are often very good at integrating into a new culture, especially the social and cultural aspects of integration. This means adapting to the local customs and daily practices. Since I arrived in the UK as a seventeen-year-old teenager, it is logical for me to devote this chapter to my social and cultural integration into the UK society.

MY FAMILY SETTING

I settled into my home in the quaint little town of Heswall.

It was a 4-bedroom detached house. My family of five (Dad, me, Stepmom, and two sisters) had grown to seven because my stepmom gave birth to two other kids before she left Nigeria. They were a boy and a girl. Therefore, I now had three sisters and a brother. It was good to have a brother because it meant I was no longer the only son in the family.

My stepmom was originally from Guyana. She was a nurse and met my father when he had major surgery at the hospital where she worked. She was the nurse in charge of his care. They fell in love, and as the saying goes, the rest is history.

As mentioned in the previous chapter, she was a genuinely nice lady who treated me like one of her own. Back in Nigeria, I addressed my stepmom as Madam because everyone addressed her that way. The driver, chef, and housemaid all addressed her as Madam. Therefore, following suit and addressing her the same way seemed natural since she was not my mother. I continued like that until one day, Dad asked me to stop addressing her as Madam. I was told to address her as 'Mum,' and I did. My stepmom liked that, and it was easy for me to call her mum, considering she was like a mum to me.

MY QUICK INTEGRATION

The first thing I adapted to was the food. My fondest memory was waking up to the smell of frying bacon and eggs, which were being prepared by my stepmom. This only happened on weekends because the parents went to work on weekdays while the children went to school. We had a regular food menu at weekends: full English breakfast (comprised of eggs, bacon, baked beans, sausages, tomatoes, and mushrooms) in the morning. It was followed by baking fresh bread and cakes in the evenings. Our home had the amazing smell of a bakery. The cake was served with custard, and these meals became my favourite. I can never forget the cake and custard. On Sunday evenings, we would have Sunday roast dinner. The food made a great impression on me.

Coming to the UK and eating these very British meals was a pleasure and something new to me even though I lived with my stepmom and the rest of the family in Nigeria, we had a chef who cooked the English dishes and traditional Nigerian dishes. I have always preferred traditional Nigerian food. My stepmom's fantastic cooking changed all that. I came to like English food as well.

On Saturday afternoons, all the kids rode with my stepmom in the car to the shops to do the weekly food shopping. My visit to the high street was one of the highlights of my week because it was always exciting to visit the shopping malls.

My dad never came with us on our shopping trips. Sometimes I stayed home with my dad to watch football.

Since I arrived in the UK in August, it was the holiday season. It was also summertime and the best time of my life because of the amazing experiences I had. That August was like 'dying and going to heaven.'

The best one was the cash gifts I received, which I was able to spend on anything I liked. The cash gifts were given to me by relatives, family friends and neighbours from Nigeria. They were quite rich. They came to stay with us usually for two or three days en route to the USA to continue their holiday. They often gave me twenty pounds, which was a lot of money back then in 1978. I went to the mall and spent the money lavishly because the twenty pounds went a long way. All I spent the money on was cakes, pies, and chocolates. I did not only spend my money at the mall, but I also spent it at the corner shops. I was fascinated with these snacks and could not get enough of them. These were food items that I was not used to in Nigeria because cakes were only eaten at birthday parties.

It never occurred to me to save the cash gift or spend it on something else other than food. I was a seventeen-year-old teenager with a sweet tooth. Looking back now, it is funny that the confectionery and snacks were the most exciting things to me at the time.

I had to adapt to the chilly winter weather too. Coming from the hot and humid tropical climate in Nigeria, which was uncomfortable most times, I liked the cool and crisp autumn weather when it came. The winter was a shock to my system at first, but I realized it was always warm indoors; being outdoors was the difficult part.

Dad made sure I had the thickest winter coats and thermal wear to keep me warm throughout the winter months.

KEY LESSONS FROM MY DAD

I had a solid relationship with my father. I think it is fair to say that my relationship with dad became even closer when I arrived in the UK. He taught me to take ownership of some important household chores like doing the laundry of his clothes and mine, which were hitherto being done by my stepmom. This pleased my stepmom tremendously, and I can imagine that doing the laundry for the whole family was a lot of work for her.

Dad was extremely strict about my ability to iron shirts and trousers to leave a crease in the right places. I struggled with ironing shirts, especially ones with cufflinks, but I mastered it.

Dad loved his Nigerian food and cooked it here in the UK since, as mentioned earlier, he had a chef cooking it for him in Nigeria. Also, my Guyanese stepmom did not know how to make Nigerian food. Dad taught me how to cook Nigerian food by asking me to assist him during the cooking process. I became better at it after watching dad do it several times.

GETTING MY GCSE & A'LEVELS

By September, the school had not released my WAEC result in Nigeria. Dad decided that I needed to continue my education in the UK so that I could attain my GCSE certificate. Dad enrolled me at Birkenhead College for further education (now renamed

Wirral Metropolitan College) for my GCSEs Non-resident and international students had to pay a tuition fee of three thousand pounds, but luckily for me, the college exempted me from paying this higher fee because my dad was a UK taxpayer. Therefore, I was allowed to register in the college as a home student to pay the lesser tuition fee of five hundred pounds.

The college was a 45-minute ride to school. I usually took the bus to school, but sometimes dad did the school run and dropped me off at school. The journey by bus was a 'culture shock,' it took me a while to adapt to it because it was vastly different from the norm in Nigeria. The UK buses had polite and helpful conductors. Everyone was so quiet on the bus and kept to themselves that I found it quite boring. I often fell asleep during my 45 minutes ride to school.

Who could blame me? I was used to Nigerian buses with rude drivers and conductors who spent most of the ride yelling and cursing at passengers. The ride was never quiet because the passengers talked over each other, quarrelling and laughing at the same time.

There would always be traders getting on and off the bus at several intervals to sell their products to anyone they could convince to buy. I found it fascinating to ride on a bus in Nigeria because there was never a dull moment. I eventually got used to the quiet bus ride by staying awake and using that time to read.

Thankfully, I did not always have to take the bus to school. The many occasions dad drove me to school were a chance for me to have a one-to-one with him. I loved it because dad seized the opportunity to regale me with stories of his personal experience at work. Most of his narratives were quite unpleasant experiences for him.

One of them was how he got a job as a clerk at UAC (United African Company) but lost it because someone framed him for money embezzlement. This incident killed his dream of becoming an accountant.

Another was when Dad was the Nautical manager responsible for inspecting ships before the company purchased them. After the inspection was diligently done and Dad produced a report, the Finance Director would veto the decision to purchase the ship without any good reason, and my Dad felt bad about it. After telling me about this particular experience, Dad would emphasise the importance of the role of a Finance Director in a company.

He explained how accountants go on to become finance directors. Dad had several stories of how well accountants are respected in the society and the good salary they earn. Eventually, I got the subtle message that the accounting profession was what Dad wanted for me. He wanted me to have the accounting career that he was 'robbed of' and unable to have. I liked the accounting profession too, and we bonded over that. However, I realised that my poor grades in mathematics were an obstacle for me. I decided to focus on that and solve that problem.

I had to sit five subjects at GCSE to qualify for admission into A' Levels. Mathematics and English language were compulsory subjects. I chose Literature, History, and Sociology as the three other subjects for my GCSE. As I mentioned in chapter two, I excelled in other subjects, as evidenced in my school report. Mathematics could be my undoing.

My first mathematics lesson was a game-changer for me. I was taught with a different approach. For example, the teacher used objects in the room to describe ANGLES, and it suddenly began to fall into place for me. I started to understand mathematics for the first time in my life. I realised then that I was not the stupid kid I thought I was, who could not understand mathematics, but that the teaching method used by my mathematics teachers in Nigeria was the problem. Similarly, I also liked the teaching method for my other subjects. I enjoyed the lessons and was good at those subjects once again.

One day, something remarkable happened in one of my maths classes that has continued to impact my life. I decided to copy a handwriting style that I found in a book. I wrote the letter 'r' in such a way that it looked like a 'c.' My teacher saw it and pronounced my name **Lance** instead of **Lanre**. I corrected him, but he ignored me and continued to call me Lance. My classmates and friends also started calling me that, and the name stuck.

I guess it was because they found it easier to pronounce the name Lance than Lanre. When my friends called my home, they would ask to speak with Lance, and Dad would say you mean Lanre. If they insist it is Lance, not Lanre, Dad told them no one called Lance lived there. It was hilarious! I have been called Lance ever since, and I like it.

I enjoyed my time at school and made many friends with kids from various ethnic backgrounds, which is a good measurement of my social integration. I also had my first girlfriend at the school, and her name was Janet.

When my GCSE results were released, I passed all five subjects, including mathematics. Instead of the usual F (fail) in mathematics, I made a C (pass). I was overjoyed at my result, and so was dad. I can confidently conclude that I integrated very well into the education system in the UK. I progressed to the A' Level to prepare for admission into the university. I chose Humanities courses, and the subjects were Economics, History, and Sociology. I passed all three subjects at A 'Level.

My dream was to study Accounting at university. However, the universities I wanted all required three As' in all the subjects or a minimum of 2 Bs' and one C. I had one B, one C, and a D in my A 'Levels. Therefore, I could not gain admission into those universities. While I was wondering what options were available to me, a few uncles and family friends advised me that a degree in accounting was risky and would restrict me to just a career in accounting.

Alternatively, a degree in business administration is broad and would pave the way for me to either get into an accounting profession or a different profession entirely. I discussed this with dad, and he agreed it was the right thing to do. Based on that, I ended up making a late application to the university to study Business administration with a finance option. I gained admission into The Liverpool Polytechnic, which has been renamed, Liverpool John Moores University.

After a year in the UK, I had adapted and integrated very well into the society. I loved the food, the weather, the educational system, and even the transport system was not so boring anymore. I was eighteen and understood that based on UK laws, I was officially an adult. Yay!

I had gained admission into the university and was excited for my adventure in university to begin. After all, I was now an adult and would enjoy some degree of independence. In Nigerian culture, parents do not consider their children as adults at eighteen. In fact, you are always a child to your Nigerian parents. So, did I get this independence I was looking forward to? Find out in the next chapter.

(Source: www.wmc.ac.uk)

From left, Me, Dad, and a family
friend at our home in Heswall

Chapter Four
Meeting My Mother For The First Time

THE TITLE OF this chapter must seem odd. How is it possible that I am meeting my mother for the first time at the age of eighteen, considering she did not give me up for adoption as a baby? Unfortunately, that is the story of my life. I do not recall meeting my mum after I was born or during my stay with my beloved grandmother. If mum visited me from the UK at the time, then I do not remember it at all.

Besides, I was having the time of my life and had no sad or unpleasant experiences that would require me to wish for my mother. Nonetheless, I occasionally asked my father questions about Mum, and I was told she lived in London. I cannot admit that I missed my mum because she was never there. Luckily for me, I had very good people in my life at different stages who filled that important motherly role. I had my grandmother, Mrs. Savage, and Mrs. Deen when I lived with each of them respectively, and they treated me like one of their own. I guess that explains why I did not grow up to have 'mother issues' because there are countless stories of men who date much older women because they have mother issues. I can confirm that I grew up to have very healthy relationships with women.

The summer after I finished my first year of A-levels, dad asked me to travel to London to meet my mum. I was so anxious and excited that I could not sleep the night before. I tossed and turned all night. I wondered what mum would be like. All I knew was that I was the spitting image of my mum. I did not know much else. I hoped my reunion with her would be a happy experience for me.

It was a three-hour train journey to London on the British Rail, which was the only overground rail in the UK in the 1970s. Dad drove me to the train station on Lime Street to board the train to London. This was my first time on a train, and I enjoyed the experience immensely. It reminded me of my flight on the plane to the UK, except for the seats, which were positioned to face each other. Dad planned and coordinated my entire trip. He made all the necessary arrangements for mum's friend, Auntie Anike, to pick me up at Euston train station. On arrival, I went to meet Auntie Anike on the concourse. She hugged me and was very warm and jovial. She treated me like someone she had known all her life. She bought me a cup of tea and tried to calm my nerves. She was a dear friend of my mum's and told me how much my mum missed me and was looking forward to the reunion with me. It worked, and I started to relax.

We got on the Victoria line train to make our way to mum's house in Brixton. The tube was fast, and we were soon at Brixton station. My first impression of Brixton was just how many black people lived there. It was like being back in Lagos. I saw many black people walking up and down the High Street. I had never seen so many of my fellow black people in one place since I arrived in the UK, and it felt good to see them. In Heswall, we were the only black family on my street. We got on the bus that would take us to Mum's house, which was only ten minutes away. My heart started to beat faster with the excitement of meeting this mystery woman who brought me into the world. I think this must be what adopted children feel when they are about to meet their biological mother for the first time.

GETTING TO KNOW MY MOTHER

My mum's house was opposite the bus stop. It was a detached house and double-fronted. A four-bedroom house with two bathrooms and two living rooms. It was like my dad's house with the same type of front garden. The front door opened, and my mother stood there. I noticed the resemblance immediately. My grandmother, auntie, and dad have told me that I looked like my mum. That day I saw her for the first time, and I could immediately see the resemblance. Yes, I was the spitting image of my mum. She hugged me and wept with the emotion of the reunion. I hugged her back happily. It felt great.

Mum asked my stepbrother and stepsister to come say hello to me. My mum had remarried after her divorce from my father as she had two little children, but she was separated from her husband at the time of my visit. This meant that I have half-brothers and half-sisters from both my mum and dad respectively. We spent some time chatting as I got to know these new members of my family. Antie Anike stayed the night, and we talked about my late grandma and reminisced about how nice and wonderful she was.

My mum worked for British Rail and usually did both day and night shifts, but she did not go to work that weekend so she could spend quality time with me. The next day, my mum took me shopping at the Brixton market. On the way, we met people in the neighbourhood who knew my mum well, and she proudly told them I was her son. Mum bought me many designer clothes, which I did not think I needed because Dad ensured I had more than enough to wear. Mum cooked all my favourite meals after I told her what they were. You can bet a full English breakfast, cake, and custard was included. It was obvious that mum was eager to do anything that would please me. I think she was overcompensating for her absence in my life for so long. It was her attempt to make up for lost time, and I decided to enjoy every moment of it.

The proverbial 'elephant in the room' was the issue of why she never visited me. I did not bring it up, but my mum decided to address it. Mum explained that the marriage ended because my Dad believed the false rumours about her. As a sailor and captain of a ship, Dad was away for long periods. Mum said she had no choice but to spend some time in the social circuit with fellow sailors' wives. All they did was party and have fun together; nothing untoward happened. However, Dad must have heard terrible things because he not only ended the marriage, he divorced her behind her back. I was unmoved by my mother's explanation and quite indifferent about it. I guess it is no surprise that I was firmly on my dad's side on this issue because it was daddy who cared for me and raised me. Nonetheless, I did not express any of this out loud. I simply listened and took it all in. I decided the best thing was to put all this behind me and enjoy my time with my mum and new half-siblings.

MY FIRST JOB

Since I was going to spend the entire eight weeks of the summer holiday with my mum, she decided I needed a job and sent me to the Brixton Jobcentre to apply. I went there and applied for a job as instructed. Those were the good old days when jobs were easy to come by. The same day I submitted my Jobcentre application, I received a call from them to attend interviews for five different jobs. I was spoilt for choice.

I attended all the interviews, and I chose the job nearest my home, a job in Stratham. The job was the role of a customer service assistant at Wilkinson, a hardware store. I was very proud of the fact that I got this job all by myself, and it was my first job. My main task was using a machine to mix paint of different colours to the customers' specifications.

I was not too fond of the job at first because it was long hours spent inside a store when I should be home doing something fun, but the job gradually grew on me, and I began to enjoy it, especially with a salary of £88 every two weeks. As Yoruba tradition demanded, I had to send my first paycheck to my father. I was ok with that because mum paid for my bus fare to work and back throughout my time on that job. My lunch at work was taken care of by Dad. He sent me his unused lunch vouchers, which enabled me to pay for nice meals without spending my salary. Dad was a Managing Director; therefore, the lunch vouchers were top quality. I enjoyed the nice meals they afforded me.

So, what did I spend my hard-earned money on? I am happy to announce that I did not spend it on cakes, pies, and chocolates like I used to. This time I spent the money partying and attending discos at Leicester Square with my friend and neighbour, Robert. We partied every weekend. Robert was a white boy who was very fashionable. He knew where to get the best Farah slacks and Hawaiian shirts, which were the vogue during that period. Robert also had a job, just like me, and we both saved up to give ourselves the best summer holiday ever. I enjoyed every bit of the eight weeks that I spent with my mum.

I eventually returned home to Heswall, but I kept in touch with my mum by telephone. We spoke often, and she remained a part of my life until she passed away 11 years ago.

Farah slacks

(**Source:** www.oshrnann.top)

Chapter Five

My University Years

UST BEFORE I started university, Dad's three years tenure at the shipping company came to an end. Therefore, the family had to relocate to Nigeria. My stepmom returned with the children immediately, while Dad stayed back to help me settle into university life at John Moore University.

Dad paid for me to get driving lessons, and I soon qualified for a driver's license. Dad allowed me to drive one of the two cars in the house. One was a sports car, which was a Ford Capri in teal blue collar, a unique colour that stood out everywhere I drove it to. I almost crashed the car once. We also had a Volvo, but it was Dad's company car. When I got better at driving, Dad also allowed me to drive the Volvo. That Ford Capri was eventually shipped to Nigeria for the family's use.

The house we lived in belonged to the company, and so was the Volvo car, so when Dad finished his tenure, he had to hand the house and Volvo car back to the company. Dad had a plan to buy a flat for me to stay, but it took longer than expected, so I had to stay at the YMCA (Young Men Christian Association, a global charity where young men can stay cheaply). I stayed there for three months,

I hated living at the YMCA. It was my first year of university and my first time living alone. The YMCA was dull, like a melting pot open to everyone.

Thankfully, the university was the opposite of boring because of the vibrant Nigerian community I found there. I was surprised to meet ten Nigerian international students at the university. I felt at home with them already, and I loved it. I joined the Nigerian community and started to hang out in the social clubs. This was where the fun at university began. There were three social clubs:

1) The Yoruba social club.

2) The Ibo social club.

3) The Nigeria Social club.

The clubs were located in L8 (Liverpool 8) on the city's fringe, specifically Granby Street and Upper Parliament Street. These clubs were for Nigerians to socialise, eat, dance, and listen to music. It was fantastic, and I enjoyed the Nigerian food of pounded yam and other delicacies. Although I was Yoruba, I hung out freely in any of these clubs. There was no discrimination on tribal grounds. During this clubbing period, I met Joe, who became my first best friend and has remained my friend ever since. Joe was much older than me and was not a student. He worked at the Nigerian High Commission.

LUCKIEST STUDENT IN THE WORLD

My accommodation woes were finally over when the flats Dad bought were finally ready for occupation. It was a three-storey building with three flats, one on each floor. Dad bought the ground and first-floor flats. The first-floor flat was a 2-bedroom flat for Dad and the rest of the family to stay when they visited the UK. The ground floor was a 1-bedroom flat, and it was mine. I was overjoyed because moving out of the YMCA into the flat was a relief for me. Dad gave me a monthly living allowance of a hundred pounds, which was a lot of money back then. It was more than enough because the food was cheap, and I could feed myself well for a week with just ten pounds. Therefore, all I needed monthly for food was about forty pounds. For some reason, Dad gave me my annual allowance of one thousand two hundred pounds in one full payment. He did not send it monthly. I believe he did that to teach me how to manage funds. I handled my finances very well because it was a generous allowance, and I never went back to Dad to ask for more money. As for my tuition, it was paid for by the government. Dad's generosity knew no bounds. He bought a small Peugeot 205 car for the family's use in the UK. He stylishly left the key in plain sight in his flat, and I found it when I was cleaning the room after Dad's departure. I interpreted this to mean the car was available for me to use, and I did. I must add that my stepmom had to use the car when she was in the UK. That was the only time I had a conflict with her, but I respectfully relinquished the car to her during those periods.

In conclusion, I had a car, a nice flat, and plenty of money to spend. I believe I have the greatest Dad in the world because he did everything to give me the best in life and ensured I did not lack anything. I love my Dad very much, which is no surprise why I do. I am fortunate to have him.

As if things weren't great already, I also had a part-time job as a DJ in the social clubs and was earning good money from it. Considering many of my classmates were doing part-time customer service jobs at retail stores, I was lucky to have a job doing something I loved. I was clubbing seven days a week, which sounds like a lot, but it did not prevent me from studying because the fear of failure kept me focused. Dad's warning was constantly on my mind. I remember his words clearly.

"Do not return to Nigeria without your kpali
(university degree)."

As much as I loved clubbing, I made time to study in the evenings before 11 pm when clubbing starts. It worked, and I was able to maintain good grades. I had nothing to worry about as a university student, which was why I considered myself the LUCKIEST STUDENT IN THE WORLD.

MY INTERNSHIP

I was cruising through university with a 2:2 result each year. In my third year, I had to do my one-year internship. I was the only black student in my year studying for a degree in Business Administration. Most of the black international students who came from Nigeria were doing the Banking and Finance degree programme.

I struggled to find a placement for my internship. Social care jobs were available to me, and I was not interested in them because my aspiration was a career in business and finance. With just two weeks left for me to find a placement, I was still looking for one. My application to most firms for the internship was rejected. I believe the colour of my skin, along with the discrimination and prejudice that came with that, was a huge factor.

Dad had to step in. He pulled some strings by using his connections with key influential people in Liverpool to secure a placement for me in an accounting firm in the Liverpool city centre. It was a placement with GAD Accountants on Castle Street.

I worked at that firm for twelve months, and I learned a lot about accounting. I was paid an annual salary of four thousand pounds, which was about four times my allowance from Dad. I was having the time of my life once again.

They were good to me at the accounting firm, and I enjoyed my internship with them so much that I asked if I could come back and work for them after graduation. They agreed on the condition that I made a 2:1 degree. I was glad to hear this because it meant I had a chance, at least. All I needed to do was study hard to get better grades. I reduced my clubbing by half to spend more time on my studies. However, I continued my part-time job as a DJ, but with fewer gigs. A year later, I graduated with a 2:1 degree. My Dad was overjoyed and came to the UK to celebrate with me. He ordered a ram from the butchers for the party and asked me to invite my friends. Joe was there with many of my other friends and coursemates.

It was the first party that I organised for myself, which was amazing. I remember that Dad never threw a party to celebrate my birthday because it was not common practice in the Nigerian culture, but I always received a birthday card from Dad every year, even when he was away in Nigeria. However, he stopped sending me birthday cards when I turned 25, which was sad because I still miss them. I digress.

I returned to GAD with my 2:1 degree as requested, and they offered me the job as promised. My journey to becoming an accountant aligned with Dad's wishes for me was about to become a reality, and I was excited.

(source: www.sliit.ik*)*

(source: www.pagabo.co.uk*)*

Chapter Six
Route To Qualification

WHEN I STARTED my employment at GAD accountants, it was a culture shock for me compared to the academic environment I was used to. Although I worked at GAD during my one-year internship, I was under supervision and training, so I did not have many responsibilities assigned to me. Returning as an accountant was a completely different experience. It was like being in a new environment entirely. This time I had responsibilities, and there were expectations of me.

BECOMING THE 'ACE ACCOUNTANT'

My first accounting lesson was that there is zero tolerance for mistakes, which I learnt in my first week. My mistake was the wrong classification of a capital expenditure. My boss was livid with anger at my mistake. I learned very quickly from that moment onwards to avoid making any more mistakes. I worked hard to learn the ropes very quickly, and I was able to avoid making further mistakes. My strategy was to ensure I understood and learned anything I was taught the first time. I got it right and never made a mistake again. I was not only good at producing error-free work, but I was also consistent at meeting the thirty hours deadline for each work assigned to me. My boss was so impressed that he nicknamed me 'Ace accountant.'

The best part of my job was the opportunity and exposure it gave me to serve clients from various industries. There were clients in construction, insurance, retail, sign-making, auto dealerships, etc. I learnt about twenty different businesses a year, and it entailed understanding each of their business systems. That was a requirement for an accountant.

I also liked the opportunity my job gave me to travel to all parts of the United Kingdom and even Jersey on all-expenses-paid business trips. It enriched my experience and knowledge as an accountant, but also my knowledge of the British culture.

I believe I became an excellent accountant because I learnt from the best. David, my boss (not his real name), was the most brilliant accountant I have ever met. He could sum up multiple columns of figures without a calculator, and when we cross-checked it, the figures were always accurate to the last digit. David had a brilliant mind. It was like magic how accurate it was.

David was not only a brilliant accountant but also a good person. This was proven when I faced racism and discrimination during my job.

ENCOUNTER WITH RACISM AS AN ACCOUNTANT

The training at GAD involved taking trainee accountants on trips to visit clients to audit their books. On one such visit, the client (a Caucasian) was surprised to see a black man as one of his auditors. The client was furious and complained openly to my boss that he did not want a black man auditing his books and did not want to ever see me in his office again. David only agreed to assign another accountant to the client because I was still a trainee at the time and quite new to the job.

A year later, we visited another Caucasian client, and this time the racism and discrimination was even worse. The client insisted that if I was not replaced with a non-black accountant, he would leave the firm and move his business to another accounting firm. This time, David did not give in to the racially motivated request. He patiently asked the client to give me a trial period. David explained how good I was and that he would replace me with a non-black accountant if he was unsatisfied after the trial period. The client reluctantly agreed.

I did such a fantastic job that the client demanded I remain his accountant for another year. During the four-year period I worked at GAD, I remained his accountant, and we became very good friends. He told David that I was professional and businesslike. Those words stayed with me ever since, and I continued to work hard to remain exactly that.

I must add here that although I was shocked at the level of racism I faced then, it was not entirely surprising to me. It was 1989, and racism was rife in the United Kingdom. It was everywhere and could not be ignored. However, I was unfazed by it because I had a father with a very successful career as a black man in the UK. His skin colour did not deter him or hinder his success. Aside from my dad, I was surrounded by many successful black professionals, and they were my role models. My biggest role model was my dad. He was brilliant at his job as a ship's captain, so I worked so hard to be equally good at my job.

My boss nicknamed me ACE ACCOUNTANT for a reason, and I was incredibly proud of that. Therefore, I felt it was the client's loss if they passed on an opportunity to work with me. This is not arrogance; just stating the fact, as was proven by my eventual acceptance by those racist clients because of my abilities and skills as an accountant.

THE ACCA QUALIFICATION

The most important qualification an accountant requires is the ACCA qualification. The acronym ACCA means ASSOCIATION OF CHARTERED CERTIFIED ACCOUNTANTS. At that time, to attain this qualification, an accountant must pass the following course examinations:

1) Level 1 - ACCA Foundation exam

2) Level 2 - ACCA Professional (1)

3) Level 3 - ACCA Professional (2)

To pass these exams, an accountant must study the following four modules:

1) **Accounting** - Learning to prepare accounts.

2) **Taxation-** Learning about the British tax system for all categories; charities, businesses, individuals, etc. How they are taxed, and the different rules for each category.

3) **Auditing -** Reviewing what another accountant has done, like retracing their steps using a checklist. We call it a walk-through test.

4) **Business Management -** Learning about leadership, motivation, etc.

The exam was immersive and rigorous. The pass mark was 51%. The ACCA examination board only allows a marginal fail which is a score between 42% - 49% in just one of the four modules. You are allowed to repeat that module, and it is called a REFERRAL. If you fail the referral, then you will be required to do the entire four modules again to attain a pass for that level. If your score from the exam is less than 42% in any of the modules, you will have to repeat all four modules again. This explains why the ACCA exam has been described as follows:

"After Brain Surgery, the ACCA Is The Most Difficult Exam To Pass"

The exams are not only difficult to pass or the qualifications to attain, it is also quite expensive. The fee is about three thousand pounds for each level of the exam. Therefore, most accountants are sponsored by their firms to write the exam.

In those days, the ACCA board gave you a period of ten years to pass the exam, although that requirement has now been relaxed. If you fail after ten years, any credit will be void and cannot be carried over to the next ten years' tranche of exams. You will have to start all over again. Although ACCA gives a time frame of ten years in which to attain the qualification, most accounting firms are not so generous, which is fair considering they take financial responsibility for the exams.

Back then, the top four accounting firms in the world (like KPMG, Andersen Consulting, Deloitte, etc.) only allow one referral. If you fail that referral, you will be fired.

Middle-level firms are less strict and more tolerant because they would give you up to three years to attain the qualification. After that, they will stop paying for the exams.

Unsurprisingly, small-level firms do not care much about these rules. They are happy to employ the accountants who were kicked out of those large firms because of the wealth of experience and skill they bring on board. They take them on and bill them per hour.

There is good news. Last year (2022), the ACCA scrapped that ten-year rule and replaced it with more flexible and somewhat more attainable guidelines for accountants to become fully qualified. (See full details below).

ACCA Time Bar Changes

Accountancy   March 11, 2022

D id you know that ACCA have relaxed their time bar rules so you no longer have 10 years from starting your studies to sitting your final exam? That means If you've previously studied ACCA papers but haven't yet progressed to full qualification, it could take just 4 papers or less for you to become fully ACCA qualified.

Previously, ACCA students were required to complete all exams within 10 years of their initial registration date. Under the new rules, exams sat at the bottom two Applied Knowledge and Applied Skills levels are ring-fenced meaning these passes are frozen and safe. Students now have seven years to pass Strategic Professional level exams – starting from the point of the first exam pass in this level.

(Source: https://www.bpp.com/insights/accatimebar)

HOW I BECAME ACCA QUALIFIED

GAD Accountants is a mid-level accounting firm. They gave their accountants three years to pass the ACCA qualification exam. We get a training contract for a period of three years, and if you do not qualify, you will have to pay for the exam yourself. The job also depended on the accountant passing these exams because they could lose their jobs if they failed to qualify.

The exam enabled all the accountants at the firm to work from the middle level upwards to top management. However, we did not all grow or advance in our individual careers at the same pace. I will cover this in more detail in the upcoming chapters.

Preparation for these exams was the most difficult part of my job as an accountant. Juggling my career and studying for the exams simultaneously was tough. GAD Accountants were supportive by giving us a total of eight weeks of study leave to prepare for the exams; two weeks in the autumn, in the winter, in the spring, and in the summer respectively. The exams took place every summer.

I made good use of my study leave and succeeded in passing most of the exams. However, I failed the Level 2 exam and had to repeat it. This was because I struggled with passing the advanced taxation exam.

It took a while for me to realise that it was because I lacked experience in international taxation. A friend gave me valuable advice that I should work for an international accounting firm to enable me to gain the experience I needed in advanced taxation. GAD was a local accounting firm because they only managed local and national businesses.

I took the advice and moved to London, where the international accounting firms were located. I got a job with an international accounting firm. It was the best decision for my career because, in just six months, I passed my advanced taxation exam to gain the much sought-after qualification as a chartered certified accountant. I finally had those four prestigious letters beside my name,

Lance Kadiri, ACCA

Chapter Seven

The Life Of A Trainee Accountant

BEING A TRAINEE accountant usually starts after graduation from university, and they are called graduate trainees. That is the norm because most accounting firms do not accept undergraduates for internships. Therefore, I was lucky to get this rare opportunity, and I have my beloved father to thank for that.

Most graduate trainee accountants prefer to focus on attaining their ACCA qualification before getting married or starting a family. This is understandable because, in the previous chapter, we explored the difficulty and stressfulness of the qualification process, which often takes place simultaneously with learning on the job.

My story is remarkably different from this because my 'journey' as a trainee accountant started during my internship at GAD Accountants. I have stated just how much I loved my internship because I could not wait to return there after graduation.

Many amazing things happened to me during my years as a trainee accountant, and it all started during my internship. When you are a trainee accountant, the world sees you as an accountant and expects you to be able to audit their books. This is even more so if you look the part

and talk the talk. I was so passionate about becoming an accountant that I went everywhere dressed in my suit with my briefcase in hand, complete with client files that I was working on.

The story about my life as a trainee accountant will not be complete without Cheryl in it. She was my girlfriend who started the accountant 'journey' with me and supported me through it all. I owe a lot to her, as would become apparent as this story unfolds.

I met Cheryl during the period of my internship. She often walked past the road in front of my home to the shops, always smiled and waved to me, and I would wave right back. She was a stunning girl, blonde and petite. I was flattered that she seemed to like me. I had the courage to ask her out on a date because I was a well-paid trainee accountant at a prestigious firm and knew I could give her a good time.

We went on a few dates and hit it off. We started a relationship soon after that. Cheryl was two years younger than me. She had a three-year-old son from a previous relationship and lived in a lovely two-bedroom council house. Since my office was near Cheryl's house, she invited me to dinner.

I was returning from work, so I turned up in my suit and with my briefcase. While Cheryl was preparing dinner, I brought out my files and started working. That showed just how passionate and focused I was about my accounting career. I guess that was the moment any woman would have dumped me for being too preoccupied with my job, but not Cheryl. Instead, she supported me and brought me coffee while I worked.

Our relationship continued like that, and I had little time for socialising. It was work, work, work for me! Cheryl was of Irish and English descent and came from a large family. Having a house to herself meant her house became a kind of 'train station' where her siblings came to hang out with their boyfriends. People were constantly going in and out of the house on a daily basis. This made it a bit difficult for us to spend quality time together; therefore, I confined myself to the bedroom most times to get some privacy. However, I did not mind that because being around a family once again felt good. I was all alone in Liverpool as Dad and the rest of the family were still living in Nigeria then. Mum was far away in London, which was quite lonely for me then.

Cheryl and her son became my family, and we were practically living together. I moved some of my clothes into her house and was having the best of both worlds. I was like a married man with a family. She cooked nice meals for me, did my laundry, and provided companionship. I also had a great relationship with her son, which was a bonus. I had no reason to live in my lonely flat anymore except when I needed to study for my exams, so I would not be disturbed.

SIGNING UP MY FIRST CLIENT

Cheryl's sister's friend had a boyfriend named Adam (not his real name) who had just opened a barber salon. Adam mentioned that he was panicking about submitting his annual accounts for the year and needed an accountant. Cheryl told him that I worked in an accounting firm, and Adam said I would be his accountant. That was how I signed up my first client.

It is important to point out that most people do not understand the fact that most accountants working in a firm may not have their qualifications yet and are on the route to qualification. Since they can work and learn on the job, the public sees them as accountants.

To Adam, I was an accountant because I worked at an accounting firm and looked the part. They always saw me bringing work home and working on those files. I was already good enough at the job to know how to file annual accounts; therefore, I could do the role of Adam's bookkeeper. Please note that as a student and an intern, I did not have a license to practice as an accountant. Under the regulations, I am not allowed to practice as an accountant. I would have to be indemnified and licensed to practice as an accountant. I found a way around that by doing the role of a bookkeeper, which I was allowed to do under the regulations.

I did an excellent job of it, and Adam was impressed. Soon after, one of Adam's customers, who owned a gardening business, mentioned that he also needed an accountant. Adam quickly recommended me to the gardener as a good bookkeeper and accountant. The gardener signed me up, and I became his bookkeeper too. This was my second client.

I signed an even bigger client; he was a referral from Cheryl's father, my future father-in-law. As a builder, Cheryl's father bought carpets from a big carpet company. When they needed a bookkeeper, Cheryl's father recommended me, which was how I signed my first major client. I became their internal bookkeeper at the company and worked there once a week. My wage was two hundred and fifty pounds a month, which was a lot of money in the 90s.

A good friend of mine once told me that I lived a charmed life. Google defines this as *"a life protected as if by magic charms: a life unusually unaffected by dangers and difficulties."*

After recounting my experiences throughout life and in this chapter, it is fair to say that my friend may be right. This is why I came to that conclusion.

I was in an interracial relationship in the 90s at a time when racism and discrimination were commonplace. My girlfriend was also a single mum. These factors were sufficient to cause untold challenges for any black man. On the contrary, my girlfriend and her family accepted me wholeheartedly and even helped me in my career.

I was also a student who was lucky to be doing an internship with a prestigious accounting firm and went on to sign clients, albeit under supervision.

At a time when I could have been lonely and miserable because my family was in Nigeria, I met Cheryl, who had a ready-made family and welcomed me wholeheartedly into her life and made me a part of it. She loved me and looked after me like a mother would. Sometimes I believe God sent me this lovely lady to look after me as compensation for not having my mother in my life during my childhood and teenage years. Or maybe God sent her to fill that 'mother figure' role that different women had filled over the years. With my stepmom in Nigeria and my mum in London, God brought Cheryl into my life at the perfect time. I was a very lucky man and living a charmed life. It gets even better. Keep reading.

STARTING A FAMILY

My relationship with Cheryl grew from strength to strength. It continued after my internship and graduation. We were officially living together at this point. She had moved from the two-bedroom council house into a flat at the edge of Liverpool City, and we were like a married couple. I drove straight there from work every day, and by 7 pm, I would have showered and had my dinner with the rest of the evening ahead of me, which I usually spent working on client files or studying for my qualification exam. Cheryl exceeded my expectations because her support was amazing. I cannot overemphasise it. She did everything a wife or even a mum would do. I was well taken care of.

After graduating from university, I was lucky to get that job at GAD Accountants. Most graduates spent the first couple of years after graduation trying to find the right job to kickstart their careers. I did not have to worry about that. At GAD, I had to 'compete' with ninety percent of colleagues who graduated from Oxford and Cambridge University. They often turned up to work in their 3-piece suits with cufflinks. Mine was always in a humble two-piece suit, but I loved cufflinks, so I started to wear them too. Unsurprisingly, I was never fazed by that competition, which was why I excelled in that job and emerged with the nickname the 'ACE accountant.'

Five years into our relationship, we had a daughter and my first child. We named her Robin Bamidele. Although we were not married at the time and the pregnancy was unplanned, it was a very happy time in my life because I loved my newborn and being a father.

However, as I recounted in the previous chapter, I was still a trainee accountant at GAD, and the job was very demanding. I had the immense challenge of learning/excelling at my job, studying for my qualification exam, and my very important domestic obligations as a father and civil partner. This was made even more tasking by the many business trips I had to make to client sites all over the UK. (I covered this in the previous chapter).

I worked all day, and I was expected to study in the evenings. I was often exhausted; all I wanted to do was rest, not study. At weekends, I looked forward to having a lie-in, but instead, I would be expected to do something fun with my partner and child (like taking Robin to her favourite toy store to buy some toys). Upon reflection, there were many expectations from me, and that came with immense pressure.

I am only human, so unsurprisingly, I struggled to meet these expectations, and my job and career had to take precedence over everything else. I could not help it because attaining that ACCA qualification was paramount in my mind. I knew that once I achieved that, the pressure would dissipate, and I would be able to spend more time with my family.

BUYING MY FIRST HOME

My preoccupation with my career started to take its toll on our relationship. Cheryl was often supportive and would bring me coffee and biscuit while I studied. Sometimes she would go out with the baby so I could study undisturbed.

However, the added responsibility of looking after a second child must have become too much for Cheryl because she snapped a few times. We had frequent arguments about this issue, and it often went like this.

'Your face is always buried in that f**king book,' shouted Cheryl.

I raised my head from the files I was working on to look at her. 'But you understand why I have to do this,' I tried to explain as I often do whenever we have this argument.

'Of course, to get the freaking accounting qualification! But Robin needs you, and I need you to help out some more,' She retorted angrily as she walked out of the room, slamming the door behind her.

My initial reaction was to be angry at her for her lack of understanding. Then I remembered all the support Cheryl had shown me through the years. I knew I could not have made it this far without her support and love. After a few such arguments, I always tried to placate her by doing something with my family or making a grand gesture that I knew would show Cheryl just how much I loved and appreciated her.

On one rare occasion, we had a nasty argument about something I cannot remember, and Cheryl threw me out of the house. She chucked my clothes out the second-floor window. I had to move into my uncle's house for a while. I did not like this, so I decided it was time to buy my own house. The one-bedroom flat Dad bought me while I was a student was too small for my growing family.

I saw a FOR SALE sign on a three-bedroom terraced house in front of my office. I liked the proximity. The house was in bad condition, but I knew it would look fantastic once renovated. The asking price was £41,000, and a required deposit of 5%. I could not afford the deposit, so I got a bank loan to pay for it. I think my job as an accountant at GAD put me in good stead to qualify for this loan. That was how I became a homeowner as a trainee accountant.

Cheryl and I made up, and she gave up her council flat to move into the house with me. However, that was after the extensive renovations were done on the property. I have Cheryl's father to thank for the renovations. He did an amazing job on the house at a minimal cost, which saved me a lot of money. I consider myself very lucky to have met this wonderful family, and I cannot thank them enough for their love and support.

That is why this chapter is somewhat of a tribute to Cheryl and her family. When I think of all I went through as a trainee accountant, I cannot help wondering if I would have continued on that path without their support since I was all alone at the time. I probably would have given up my ambition to become an accountant.

I must mention that Dad was against my relationship with Cheryl initially. He disapproved of me having a Caucasian partner or wife. He wanted me to marry a black woman and told me that several times. I ignored his advice and remained with Cheryl. Many years later, we got married, were blessed with a son, and named him Kieran.

CONCLUSION

The life of a Trainee Accountant is fraught with countless challenges, as you have read above. My situation was a peculiar one as I did not have the physical presence and support of my family behind me at the time, but I was fortunate to meet Cheryl and her family. Thankfully, it led to the signing up of my first client, the birth of my first child, and buying my first home.

I guess the moral of this tale is that you can overcome the challenges faced by a trainee accountant if you have the love and support of your family behind you. If you do not, I would advise focusing on attaining your qualification before starting a family because you will have enough difficulties on your plate without the added pressure of your domestic obligations.

With my first child Robin, at age two.

With Cheryl, Kieran, Robin, and a friend having fun.

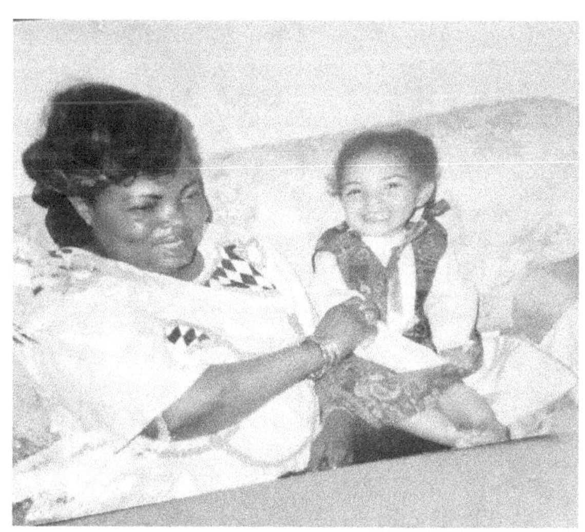

My mother with Robin.

With my first son, Kieran.

My first child, Robin. All grown up

Chapter Eight

The Professional Struggle Begins

MY PROFESSIONAL STRUGGLE started with me trying to get a job in London. I could not get a job in London with a white firm. I attended over twelve interviews, and they usually lasted about ten minutes. The questions were never about accounting. Instead, they were chit-chats about Africa or where I come from. I always departed those interviews, knowing they would never take me to the next stage of the recruitment process or give me the job. The discrimination and racism were so blatantly obvious that if they offered me the job, I would have turned it down anyway.

The recruitment agencies realised that the Jewish firms were prepared to employ anyone with the right qualifications and experience. Therefore, they started to

present my CV to Jewish firms. It is important to point out that there were more white firms in the home counties, like Dover, Kent, Bromley, etc., than in London, where I wanted to work. Since I was not prepared to travel more than forty-five minutes to work, I had no choice but to keep looking for work.

I eventually got a job with HR and Co Accounting firm in London. After I qualified, the senior partner in the firm, Mr R, told me we were both the same now. Wow! I was surprised to hear that and did not understand exactly what he meant because this man had sixty years of accounting experience behind him. However, I was glad to hear that he considered us EQUALS. It gave me faint hope that I would not suffer from racism and discrimination at that firm.

My first assignment was to audit the account of a very successful author–a millionaire based in Guernsey for tax purposes. Guernsey is popularly known as one of many tax havens. (a tax haven is a country or independent area where taxes are <u>levied</u> at a low rate). I had to travel to Guernsey to carry out the assignment. We flew there and stayed in a luxurious hotel. I had a fantastic time and thought THIS WAS THE LIFE!

I have written about visiting client sites in previous chapters to conduct an audit, so I think it would be good for me to shed some light on what that entails because it is a key part of accountants' work. The accounts are usually sent days before the visit. The accounts were prepared by the company's chief accountant (some companies do not have in-house accountants, so we have to double as the accountant and the auditors).

The chief accountants of these companies were usually people with decades of experience, yet we auditors with less experience are sent to check the accounts they prepared. Therefore, I usually found these auditings were a learning experience for me.

Auditing these books could best be described as an analytical review to see if it gives it a TRUE and FAIR view of the company's financial activities. That is, the assets and liabilities. This is done by taking a random test sample of five percent of the transactions as a representative of the overall accounting record to prove that what you have been given is a true picture of the financial statement.

Auditing is no longer a requirement for all businesses now because the threshold has been raised. The Companies Act 2006 stipulates that SMEs (small and medium-sized companies) are no longer required to have an audit unless ten percent of the shareholders request it.

My employer, HR and co, had famous people from the Arts and Literary world as clients. However, the clients were represented by their agents. Therefore, all our dealings were with the agents who made all the decisions, which is why most artists are often ripped off by their agents. The agents were in full control of everything and were the ones who recommended accountants, lawyers, doctors, etc, to those they managed.

Another offshore client based in Guernsey that I audited was the set designer of a globally famous west end and Broadway show, which is still generating plenty of income today since its creation in the 90s. The client was able to negotiate a small percentage of the royalties, and that is how he became a millionaire because the theatre show is still being staged in Theatres worldwide. We dealt directly with the agent for this client. Jewish firms were very good at networking because that is how they are able to sign on such famous clientele.

The firm also had regular clients like big construction firms who built skyscrapers and estates in the UK. I preferred dealing with the more glamorous and exciting clients in the Art and Literary world. It was fascinating!

MEETING MY FIRST BLACK ACCOUNTING CLIENT

In all the years that I worked at GAD Accountants in Liverpool City as an accountant, I never came across a black client. Not once. How was that possible, even back then in the 90s? Is it that black people did not own businesses? My answer would be No because they definitely did. However, black businesses tend to do business differently. When we consider the fact that people like to patronise accountants that look like them and that there were barely any black accounting firms at the time, the black businesses probably found a different way to meet their accounting needs. I think black businesses need to have more faith in being accountable because, back in the 90s, they were not.

The black clients I met at HR and Co were actors and actresses, but only a few of them. It felt good to serve clients from my own ethnic background. I realised these black clients would need an accountant who looked like them because people gravitate towards accountants that look like them since they have to share some very confidential information about their spending patterns and other private information. Therefore, I started to study the

peculiarities of that market segment, so I would know how to provide them with the right consulting services. There were hardly any black firms at the time. The black accountants that were lucky to get a job worked at Jewish firms.

NO CAREER PROGRESSION

I worked at HR and Co for three years and made no progress in my career during that period. Junior colleagues were assigned to me for training. I watched as these junior colleagues were made salaried partners as soon as they attained their accounting qualifications. A salaried partner is a partner who has little stake in the business but also receives a salary. When I qualified, all I got was a handshake and a meaningless speech about being equals. Actions they say speak louder than words. Evidently, I was never treated equally to the partners; instead, I was treated worse than the trainee accountants.

It was gut-wrenching to experience this over and over again. To see my junior colleagues become partners with their names on the letterhead. I guess they did not want my African name on the letterhead of a Jewish firm. That being said, I could understand why they discriminate. The white firms also do not make Jewish employees partners in their firms. Therefore, the Jewish firms were practising reverse discrimination. Everyone was doing it back then in the 90s. I think a Black or Asian accounting firm would probably do the same by making only black or Asian employees partners in their respective accounting firms.

The reason Jewish firms thrive in accounting is because they have lots of Jewish entrepreneurs who need accountants. They also have big businesses, which is the most important thing for the growth and stability of an accounting firm.

For a black accounting firm to thrive, they would need big black firms that did not exist then. Most black professionals worked as IT consultants or management consultants, and these were mainly the ones who required accountants. They were not big businesses that could sustain an accounting firm. Thank God the situation is much better today in 2023. There are big black businesses all over the UK today, especially in the hospitality and food industry.

No matter how good you were as a black accountant, you would be stuck in the same position. When I complained about the lack of career progression, I was always given a slight pay rise, probably to shut me up. The best you could get back then was an inflationary salary increase according to the inflation rate, so your income is not devalued. This increase was usually about five percent. (Not much has changed since then). It dawned on me that if I wanted a better salary at least, I had to change jobs and move to another accounting firm, which was what I did.

MY ENTRY INTO THE WORLD OF
ACCOUNTING IN SPORTS & ENTERTAINMENT.

My new employer was also a Jewish firm, but they had even more famous and exciting clientele this time because they were sports and entertainment clients. I met famous footballers, and some of them were black as well. Meeting these A-Listers and understanding how an accountant can help them was even more exciting. The biggest one was an England goalkeeper. I was in awe and so excited to meet him that I almost collapsed. Lol! I realised then that the accounting profession could be really exciting.

One of the accountants in the firm was responsible for bringing in these top clients, which was admirable. I was desperate to get a footballer client too. The closest I got was the son of my father's friend. He was discovered at the age of fifteen and signed up by a Premier League football club. I was excited when I heard this and believed I could sign him up since I was already his father's accountant. Unfortunately, I could not. His father said the boy's football agent made all the decisions and had already signed him up with another accounting firm. I realised then that the football world was like a 'mafia' world. The agents' fee was about 25 - 30% of everything the footballers earned, and that was how they ripped off the players.

The agents were in complete control and recommended the lawyers and accountants to the stars they represented. The Jewish firms were good at networking with these agents, which was how the Jewish firms cornered the market.

I wanted an agent on my books to enable me to sign up footballing clients. To be a football agent, you have to register with FIFA (**Fédération Internationale de football association**), and the fee is one hundred thousand dollars. I worked with an aspiring agent to raise the registration fee, but we could not, and the guy had to give up.

Doing business with those famous black clients gave me the idea to branch out on my own because I recognised that there was black clientele out there that I could be of service to. I heard how a famous black boxer squandered $300m of his money. When I heard such things, I had this big dream to help them because I understood the black culture and spending patterns. I knew they had a problem linked to their lifestyle; too many hangers-on, money wasted on luxury goods and designer clothes. Most of them grew up poor in the ghetto and often got carried away with so much money, and they spent it foolishly and eventually became broke quite quickly or soon after their sports career ended.

PREVENTED FROM LEARNING
HOW AN ACCOUNTING FIRM OPERATES

I was at this second Jewish firm for two years. During that time and even in my previous job, I was only allowed to work in the accounting and auditing department out of the six departments in an accounting firm. Namely:

1. Accounting

2. Audit

3. Tax

4. Estates and Trust

5. Payroll

6. Business Development or Consulting.

Most accountants start in accounting and auditing but never move to the other departments unless they are made a partner. Therefore, you never get the chance or privilege to understand how an accounting firm operates. As a partner, you get this privilege that a black accountant never gets, and that means you will never be allowed to advance in your career or learn enough to start your own accounting firm if you want to. You are STUCK and exactly where they want you to be.

Only prospective partners are sent to do the tax training and qualification exam. The tax was a speciality area, and you had to pass the Institute of Taxation exam to attain the qualification. In hindsight, maybe I should have gone out of my way to get this qualification because my employer would have been forced to allow me to work in the tax department. I needed tax experience but could not get one at the firm. I was lucky to get a part-time job as a tax assistant, which I did at weekends. (This is called Moonlighting – to have a secret second job, typically at night, in addition to one's regular employment). I thank God for that part-time job because I would never have had that exposure to learn how to do taxes.

I also indicated an interest in becoming a trainer in the firm after sitting through some training classes organised for the firm. I was often the only one able to answer accounting questions that even my senior colleagues and partners could not answer. I was passionate about it and saw it as a career path I could carve for myself at the firm. They declined my request and told me to stick with accounting and auditing.

RESIGNATION

Based on all the professional struggles I have narrated above, it was not difficult to arrive at the conclusion that resignation from the firm was the best course of action for me at the time. One more reason I decided to leave was the fact that I was only allowed to audit the same clients year in and year out. It became boring for me because I was auditing the same businesses. Some variety of clients or new ones would have been nice.

I started to make plans for my imminent resignation. I decided to go into partnership with another accountant. I took out a six-month lease on a small office space, and every evening, I would go to work there to see my clients. I had signed up about ten clients at that point. I was doing a good job with these clients and enjoyed being my own boss. I knew I was ready for that big step.

I was in Nigeria in December 1999 for Christmas. The excitement of the upcoming millennium, the year 2000, was trending. All we heard in the news was Y2K. (the shorthand term for "the year 2000."). Everyone was talking about it. I decided it was the perfect time for a new beginning. On my flight back to the UK in January 2000, I wrote my resignation letter and submitted it to my boss on resumption at work. My boss did everything to convince me to stay, but I refused. I was done and ready to take my accounting career into my own hands.

I believed in my abilities and knew I could do better than that dead-end job. I knew I could succeed on my own, so I went for it. After all, I was the ACE ACCOUNTANT; otherwise, my boss would not have tried so hard to retain me. I gave up on being an employee and never looked back.

CONCLUSION

This is my advice. Learn from my above experience and mistakes. You must go out of your way to learn what you need for your professional development. Network as much as you can. Do some moonlighting if you have to because that would give you the added skill and experience you need. Do not wait or rely on the firm to give you all you need for your career, or you will be disappointed. Otherwise, you may end up stuck there for decades doing the same thing and never making a partner or progressing in your career.

Chapter Nine

Starting My Own Firm

LANCE LINCOLN & CO ACCOUNTANTS

ON 3RD FEBRUARY 2000, I started to work in my own accounting firm, and it was a partnership with a man named Lekan. He was introduced to me by our mutual friend, Dunzor, whom I met in accounting school. Lekan and I clicked immediately after we met. It was like we had known each other all our lives. We put up the capital to start the firm. It was a partnership, and we named it LANCE LINCOLN & CO. Although we did not know who the '& CO' would be, we left it that way and kept that position open.

Lekan had a restaurant on Kilburn High Street, and we used the two rooms on the top floor for the offices. Lekan was an accountant from Nigeria who relocated to the UK for greener pastures. Although he was not interested in practising accounting in the UK, he was a business opportunity in having an accounting business, so he became a part of it only in name. Lekan was more committed to running his profitable restaurant and property business.

Although I came into the firm with ten clients, their business was too small to generate enough monthly income for me.

Therefore, I struggled financially in the first few months of starting independently. My previous salary at the Jewish firm was a gross annual salary of thirty-five thousand pounds, which was about two thousand four hundred pounds monthly net salary. My mortgage on the two-bedroom flat that I bought and where I lived was four hundred pounds a month. The solution was to take a lodger who was paying half of my mortgage because the rent was two hundred pounds. My wife and two children stayed back in Liverpool.

I had no guaranteed income. The lease on the office premises was fifty pounds a month, and there were months when I could not even afford that. This showed my financial struggle at the time. I thought I would have clients in the sports and entertainment industry since I had a good experience in that sector, but that did not happen.

All I wanted was to generate an income of about one hundred thousand pounds. I figured since I was able to clock three hundred thousand pounds annually for my employer, I would be happy to make a third of that income for myself. It turned out to be more difficult than I ever dreamed it would be.

GROWING MY BUSINESS

The Y2K issue that all computers would malfunction on 31st December 1999 created a boom in the IT job market two years earlier (since 1998) as organisations frantically prepared for the Y2K effect. It made a lot of Nigerian professionals go into the IT business. They earned their money from 1998 - 2000. There were many of them in the IT industry at that time, and they were earning a really good wage of £300 - £400 per day. These IT Consultants were the main customers who patronised Lincoln's restaurant.

Lekan heard them complaining about their accountants and how unhappy they were with their Indian and white accountants. Lekan seized the opportunity and persuaded them to move their accounts to our firm upstairs. Most of these professionals looked up to Lekan and respected him. He was a successful businessman with a restaurant and a string of properties to his name. Therefore, any advice or recommendations from him had to be taken seriously.

This was the beginning of our change in fortune. All I needed was for them to sit before me, and I would close the deal. We signed up many Nigerian clients, both male and female, in the IT industry. They were so happy with our service that they referred their colleagues to us. They needed an accountant to help them prepare their accounts for mortgage applications, and I was able to help them with that.

One of my female IT Consultant clients introduced an Indian man named Vijay to me. Vijay signed up with our firm and became a blessing to our business. He was like a 'torchbearer' for my business because he recommended so many clients to us.

This is a thank you and a tribute to Vijay, who has been my good friend ever since.

The location of our office was an advantage for the business because it was not in London city. Most accounting firms were in the city, which was difficult for clients to drive into. Since our clients were mostly in and around the Kilburn area or outside the city, we were easily accessible to them, and they were happy to come there after work.

THE BUSINESS SIGN -
'THE GOOSE THAT LAID THE GOLDEN EGGS'

We had a double-sided triangular sign for our business. One side of the sign had the word ACCOUNTING written on it, and the other side had the word TAXES written on it. We mounted this sign on the pavement outside the restaurant. It was like 'magic' or a 'lucky charm' because it attracted many walk-in clients to our firm. It was the best one hundred and fifty pounds I ever spent.

It started with other restaurant customers, not just the IT professionals. Then came those supplying goods to the restaurant. They saw the sign on the pavement and walked in to discuss their accounting and taxation needs. We were able to sign up most of them. I soon realised that the Kilburn area was full of people from all ethnic backgrounds because those were the people who came through the door—the Irish, Australians, New Zealanders, English, etc.

Our pavement business sign also attracted some Irish builders. The builders and electricians are usually self-employed and uneducated about taxation and accounting. The British government devised a scheme to help them and all merchants. It was called the CIS - Construction industry scheme. It stipulated that the construction firms (the contractors) must withhold twenty-five percent of the payment for the tradesmen (the sub-contractors).

The first Irish builder that walked into our office came in with six years' worth of CIS certificates. Back then, claiming up to six years' worth of CIS was possible. I was able to help him process the claim, and the builder received a payment of fifteen thousand pounds, and we received our fee of thirty percent of that sum, which was four thousand five hundred pounds. It was our biggest single fee from one client, and we were quite excited to receive that.

The Irish builder was so happy with our service that he invited me to the pub for a drink. Although I do not drink alcoholic beverages, I went along and had a glass of fruit juice. At the pub, we met some friends and colleagues of the Irish builder, and I was able to sign up another five clients through him.

Another amazing client was a lady from New Zealand. She said she had seen our window business sign several times while riding on the bus past our office. She was an IT professional and walked in one day to sign up with us. She was so happy with our services that she brought in a trailer load of her friends and colleagues who were immigrants from New Zealand and Australia with three-year-visas to work and earn good money.

I must point out here that there was very little discrimination because I was able to sign up walk-in customers from all ethnic backgrounds. I successfully signed up ninety-five percent of the walk-in customers. Only a handful of the walk-in clients, which was about five percent, refused to sign up with us. I believe they saw the name of our firm and came in expecting to see Caucasians but met a black accountant instead.

My advice to black professionals out there is that your training, skill, and experience are all that matters because what a client really wants is a good accountant who can solve their accounting and taxation problems. Therefore, if you are good at what you do, the clients will come, and the business will thrive. It also helps that when a client walks into an accounting firm, they are already desperate for help with their taxes or filing their accounts.

Our business grew from ten clients to over a hundred. I was happy to be earning an income of over six hundred pounds a week, equivalent to my previous monthly salary at the Jewish firm. Lekan was an amazing business partner because he allowed me to keep all the income. His decision was based on the fact that I was the one providing the accounting services and not him. He only took payment for the rent of the office space.

Our lucky pavement sign disappeared one day. We discovered the council removed it, and we never got it back. We had received several requests and warning letters to remove the sign from the pavement because it was a health hazard, but we ignored the warning letters because the sign led so many clients to us and generated plenty of business for us. We were sad to lose that sign.

OUR BIG BREAK

Our big breakthrough came in 2001 in the form of the ILA (Individual Learning Account). The government realised that there was no problem with the anticipated impact of the Y2K, so they decided to roll out broadband All over the country. The government gave each adult from the age of eighteen a two hundred pound ILA voucher to pay for training on how to use computers. Lekan is a very smart businessman who spotted this business opportunity immediately. He discussed the strategy with me. He wanted us to register a computer training company which he would manage. Since I was responsible for the accounting business, Lekan would handle the training. We argued about the sharing formula. I wanted it to be 50-50 or fifty percent each. Lekan said that since he left most of the income from the accounting business to me, it was only fair that he gets a higher percentage of the earnings from the computer training business.

I had to agree to this because I wasn't going to be doing the training with Lekan. This seemed fair enough, so I agreed to it. At the end of the day, I was only lending my name to the business without doing the work, and for that, I would be paid a handsome forty percent of the earnings. It was the same way Lekan lent his name to the accounting firm but did not do the work and only received the rent for the office premises. It was clear that I was getting a better deal.

I registered the business as agreed, and we commenced operations. Lekan went to the job centre to give out his flyers for computer training. He promised tea, sandwiches, and a four-week training. Many signed up with Lekan and his training partner. They turned up at our training centre with their vouchers and the training commenced. Every voucher we received was money for us. Some completed the training, while many dropped out and stopped attending the training sessions. This bothered me because I wondered what would happen if the government decided to investigate the non-completion of the training for students for whom we have received payments.

Three months into the training, we received payment for all the ILA vouchers we had processed, and the cheque was for the sum of sixty-eight thousand pounds. We were overjoyed with excitement. Our biggest cheque ever received by the firm was fifteen thousand for the CIS payment. This was much bigger. Lekan went to the bank with me to process that cheque; my forty percent share was about twenty-eight thousand pounds. We had finally made it because that was a lot of money in 2001.

We made this sum of money within three months, meaning more money would come. Unfortunately, I got scared and decided to pull out of the ILA business. My reason was simple. I was concerned that we received payments for people who did not complete their training. Knowing the British government, they had a habit of coming back years later to claw back any overpayments. I figured if they could do that for genuine benefit payments, then it was only a matter of time before they came chasing us for overpayments on the ILA.

Lekan tried to talk me out of pulling out, but I was adamant and did not listen to him. It was a huge risk that could jeopardise my ability to practice as an accountant. It did not bear thinking about because my profession and career were my means of livelihood; therefore, it was everything to me. I did not want my name involved in it anymore because of the perceived risk.

Lekan eventually accepted my decision, and I agreed to register another computer training company under his name. This caused a rift in our friendship, and we had to part ways. I left the firm and moved out of the office premises to form another partnership with two other accountants. I shall cover this in the next chapter.

Surprisingly, there were no repercussions from the government. Lincoln and his friend continued the training and made a fortune, about five million pounds. Lincoln was not the only one doing this business at the time. There was news of other businesses earning ten million or more from the ILA business. Lincoln went on to build an estate of thirteen flats in Ikoyi, the most sort after residential location in Lagos, Nigeria. That could have been me if I had stuck with the ILA business.

Lekan and I reconciled years later, and we are still great friends today. I have a lot to thank him for. He brought so much business into our accounting firm. If I had not met Lincoln when I did, I do not know what would have happened to my business at that time. I call it divine intervention, and I thank God for his mercy upon me.

Chapter Ten

A New Chapter In My Life

MOVED OUT of the Kilburn office I shared with Lincoln into another office down the road. For a brief period, I was on my own but still practising under the partnership name Lance Lincoln & Co. Needless to say, I took that Window sign with me, and it was business as usual. It did not make much difference in the day-to-day running of the business because it was always just me doing the accounting business anyway, as we established in the previous chapter. Lincoln was happy for me to keep practising with the partnership name, so I carried on. I had over a hundred clients at this point, and I was happy.

Soon after, I arranged a loose association with another accountant named Felix Taggart. He was a mixed-race gentleman with a Scottish father and a Nigerian mother. Everyone called him Taggart, and he was very jovial and popular. A well-liked man. He was a taxation specialist working for an Australian firm.

The nature of our loose association was for him to refer his clients who needed accounting services to me, and I will refer my taxation clients to him. Taggart referred many clients to Lance Lincoln & Co, where he provided taxation services. This was a great arrangement, and we continued to work like that for a while.

THE END OF MY MARRIAGE

It was 2002, and my family and I had been living apart for a few years because my wife and children were still back in Liverpool. I simply buried myself in my work, which was how I coped with the loneliness. My family remained in Liverpool because my wife, Cheryl, wanted to live near her family, and London would be too far away.

However, it bothered me that my children would grow up without a broader perspective on life because all they knew was the lifestyle in Liverpool. I needed to broaden their horizon. Therefore, I took the drastic decision to sell my house in Liverpool as a way to force my family to move down to London and live with me finally. I missed them and needed them with me. I was also missing out on their growing-up years because Robin was already fourteen, and Kieran was nine.

Selling the house worked, and my family moved to London, and I was able to get my children into a Catholic school nearby. It was actually easier than expected because they were baptised Catholics and had been attending catholic schools in Liverpool. Remarkably, Kieran started school two days after they arrived in London.

Although living in London was fun for the children, it was not the same for my wife, Cheryl. It was boring for her as she had little to do there. Her life usually involved helping her parents and spending a lot of time with them. She missed them terribly and wanted to return to Liverpool to be near them. I tried to convince her to consider what would happen when her parents passed away and she could not visit them anymore. What will she be doing in Liverpool then?

Cheryl ignored my advice, and in 2004, just two years later, she moved back to Liverpool with the children. That was it for me. The marriage could not continue after that. I needed my wife and children with me, and I could not build a successful accounting business in a small town like Liverpool, where racism, prejudice, and cultural differences were still rife. Our interracial marriage was a challenge in Liverpool and was still unaccepted by most people. In London, a metropolitan community, we stood a better chance of a peaceful marriage and successful business. It was a no brainier.

It was sad for me that my marriage had to end. Cheryl was very close to my parents. She would drive Dad everywhere he wanted to go when he visited the UK from Nigeria. She was best friends with my mother, and they were not happy with the news that our marriage had collapsed, but they came to accept that it was inevitable based on the situation as it was.

I coped with this difficult period in my life by doing what I do best, burying myself in my work. I had the support of good friends who were always available to hang out with me and provide company when I needed it. My best friend, Tola Johnson, was there for me throughout and helped me through this difficult time. Another close friend was Mr and Mrs Lawrence. I visited their home almost every week to hang out with them.

A NEW PARTNERSHIP -
LANCE TAGGART & WEST IS FORMED

2004 also brought me an opportunity for a fresh business partnership. It all started when Taggart was made redundant by the Australian firm he worked for. The timing could not be more perfect because Taggart had brought in so many clients to my firm that it was the natural progression for our business relationship.

I invited Taggart to form a partnership with me, and he accepted. Since we had both the accounting and taxation side of the firm covered, we needed another partner to cover the marketing and networking side of the business. After observing the value that good networking and marketing brought to the Jewish accounting firms I worked for in the past, I knew it was imperative that we did that at our firm too.

Taggart found the perfect person for the position. It was a man named Deji West. He was a dynamic and well-spoken gentleman who could penetrate any ethnic group. He was gifted with the right personality and skills to do it. West fitted into the partnership perfectly.

We decided to choose a befitting name for our partnership, but it was more difficult than we expected. After two weeks of deliberation, we could not agree on the right name. We knew we had to use our Own English or Western names because it would help us to break into the UK market. It is what it is, and we had no choice but to conform. Using our Nigerian names would not have helped us at that time as it would prove a barrier to our business growth. This explains why my previous firm was named Lance Lincoln & Co, not Lanre Lekan & Co.

We eventually agreed on the name Lance Taggart & West since the acronym LTW was similar to the then-popular LWT - London Weekend Television. We moved to a beautiful office premises and had a great partnership. It was good to work in the same office again with other accountants.

A NEW WIFE AND MORE CHILDREN

Six months after my marriage ended, I turned up at my friends' home, the Lawrences, and a young woman named Omolara opened the door to let me in. She was the junior sister of Mrs Lawrence, who had just moved to the UK from Nigeria. My first impression of Omolara was that she had to be a married woman with kids because she looked so responsible and reserved. She was also quite religious. Pursuing a relationship with her did not cross my mind at that point. We both did not see it coming because she used to call me Uncle Lance, as our age gap was over ten years.

I later discovered that Omolara was an entrepreneur in Nigeria with a successful fashion design business. She was not married but had a boyfriend who lived in a different country.

After hanging with the family several times, I became interested in Omolara. I learnt her long-distance relationship was not going well, and so I made my move.

I knew she liked going to church, so our first date was an invitation to a church service. To my surprise, Omolara invited her junior sister along on the date, which I found quite funny. If I had spent my dating years in Nigeria, I would have realised this was the common practice for young women over there. They often invite a friend or relative to come with them on a date as a sort of chaperone until they are comfortable enough to be alone with the man or when they like him enough.

The date went well, and we had several more and were soon in a full-blown relationship. I was determined to win her heart and steal her from her quarrelsome relationship with her long-distance boyfriend. I showered with love, attention, and gifts. I surprised Omolara one day by furnishing her bedroom with some luxury gadgets from Curry's. Omolara and the whole family were impressed with my commitment to the relationship.

A few months after we started dating, I asked Omolara to move in with me, and she agreed. I think living with her sister and the husband was uncomfortable and meant to be a temporary arrangement. Therefore, Omolara was happy to move out and live with the man she loved. A year later, we welcomed our first child, our son, and named him Timi. This was a beautiful new chapter in my life.

I started to process my divorce from Cheryl, which was soon finalised. I married Omolara in 2007, and we have been together ever since and have had a fantastic marriage. We have been blessed with three more children, and they are girls. We named them Tobi, Tomi, and Tami respectively.

Married life with Omolara and the kids has been everything I wanted it to be, living with my family and watching my children grow. Having a hardworking wife running her own business and, best of all, practising Christians who walk in faith with God almighty. It has been a true blessing to me.

I must pay tribute to my wife here for her tremendous support over the last nineteen years. What I appreciate the most about Omolara was something she did early on in our relationship when we moved in together. It was a rare gesture for a married woman and not often seen in our culture. She saw I was paying all the bills (mortgage, utilities, feeding, clothing, and other personal care), and she said these words to me,

> *"I know I cannot match the income you bring*
> *into our home that takes care of all our bills,*
> *but one thing I can take care of is the food bill.*
> *I shall take ownership and responsibility for*
> *feeding in our home from now onwards."*

I was blown away by this statement and loved Omolara even more for it. Soon after, she got a job, did exactly as she promised, and started to pay for our feeding, which has remained like that ever since. Nineteen years and four children later, Omolara is still feeding our household, and I cannot express how much it means to me and how much I appreciate that because my children eat a lot of food.

I also love Omolara's entrepreneurial spirit. She has been running several businesses over the years (including a restaurant), which she juggles with raising four children (two of them being teenagers) is no mean feat. She is also heavily involved in church activities, which we now do together. We are both church ministers.

My wife's moral support is priceless; my accounting business has grown from strength to strength ever since we met. I am truly blessed and thankful to God for my life and marriage. I have been blessed with six children, and thanks to Omolara for building a beautiful relationship with Robin and Kieran. She is a great stepmother to them, so we have become one big, happy, close-knit family.

THE END OF LANCE TAGGART & WEST

In 2007, the same year I remarried, our firm had to dissolve the partnership because we all wanted different things. We had been together for three years and had an excellent and productive partnership, but the time came to make tough decisions about the future of the business.

West was never fully committed to the accounting business because he had a day job as a SAP consultant, earning him about five hundred pounds daily. That was enough money for him not to bother about our accounting business too much. Nonetheless, he performed his role as the marketer and networker for the firm. An opportunity came for him to relocate to Nigeria and take up a job offer from an oil and gas company. He jumped at the opportunity and left the UK, resigning from the partnership.

Taggart had a different vision for the accounting firm and a change in direction for the company, which was entirely different from mine. This made it difficult for us to continue working together. Therefore, Taggart left to set up his own firm and practised accounting for many years. He was actually the only partner I had who was as committed to the profession as I am.

My two partners left me with a long office lease without considering how I would handle the contractual obligations. Luckily for me, the landlord was gracious enough to allow me to get out of the lease agreement, and I gladly moved out of the premises and started to work from home.

I was now at a crossroads. I had tried running a partnership in two different firms, and it was clear that what I could get was either a partnership with people who were not interested in practising the profession or those who wanted to practice it in a way I did not want to. I was tired of this START AND STOP debacle that I have found myself on two occasions in my business career.

This was the perfect time for me to go it alone, just like many accountants were doing in London and all over the UK. I was not alone anymore because I had the love and support of a good wife and family beside me, so I knew the sky was the limit.

I have remained good friends with my former partners. We talk all the time. Sadly, Taggart passed away in 2021 due to complications from the Covid-19 virus infection. May his soul rest in peace.

Me and Omolara at our wedding.

With my best man and best friend, Tola Johnson, at my wedding.

Timi, my second son and first child with Omolara

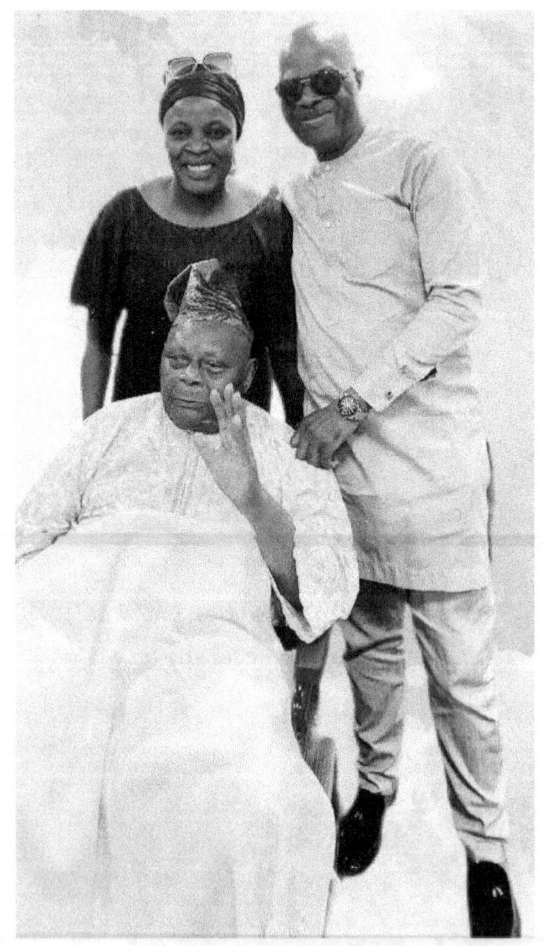

With Dad and Omolara on Father's Day 2023

Chapter Eleven

The Birth Of My Spearmans Business Empire

MY HOUSE BECAME my office, which lasted for a year (2007 - 2008). I created a home office with some of the furniture when the partnership ended, and our lease was cancelled.

However, the rest of the furniture was too much to fit into my garage, which was not surprising because we had quite a large office with three partners and five employees. Taggart walked away from our partnership without taking any furniture. He wanted a clean break and a fresh start, so he bought a new office and furniture. I ended up shipping the rest of the furniture to Nigeria.

GOING IT ALONE

I had spent the last seven years operating my business as a partnership, which had many advantages but also came with the disadvantage of doing business with people who do not share your business vision wholeheartedly or are not interested in doing accounting at all.

This resulted in short-lived partnerships, as my last two partnerships have been. It also meant a lot of money wasted on stationery and websites that had to be discarded because they could no longer be used. How about the expensive lease of our last office space that was eighteen thousand per year? I hate to contemplate what would have happened if I could not get out of that lease when Taggart and West left me in the lurch and just walked away.

I had enough and wanted to be in a position where I made all the decisions for the direction of my firm. I needed stability and consistency in my business. I had over a hundred clients; therefore, I was starting from a position of strength. This was going to be different and much better. I could feel it in my bones, and it was exciting.

SPEARMANS IS BORN

I needed the perfect name for my business, which had to be so generic that I would not have to change it. It required careful consideration.

Everyone has called me Lance since my teenage years in Liverpool. My friends in Nigeria injected Spearman into the name and called me Lance Spearman, based on a fictional character.

"Lance Spearman (aka «The Spear») is a fictional character created in 1968 by Drum Publications. The Adventures of Lance Spearman was published in a weekly photo comic that went by the title African Film in East and West Africa and Spear Magazine in South Africa and was featured in over one hundred and fifty issues.

Lance Spearman was widely regarded as the James Bond of English-speaking Africa from Kenya on the East Coast to South Africa and across the West Coast in Nigeria and Ghana. At its zenith, Lance Spearman had over half a million fans[4] across the continent until the series was discontinued in 1972.

The fictional Spear is a sophisticated African super-spy, detective, and superhero all rolled into one,[6][7] who sports a goatee, smokes expensive cigars, drinks Whisky on the rocks, and dresses in well-tailored suits complete with a bow tie and a Panama hat. Spear likes buxom women and drives the Corvette Sting Ray] Spear is an expert marksman and is skilled at karate and boxing."

(Source: https://en.wikipedia.org/wiki/East_Africa**)**

My friends must have seen something in me that reminded them of this fascinating character. I loved the name Spearman and decided to adopt it for my business. I saw it as fate presenting me with a solution to my search for the perfect business name.

I added an 's' to the name, which was how my business name was formed - SPEARMANS. I registered it, and it has become the name for the various arms of my business ever since.

A SPECIAL FOCUS ON BUSINESS CONSULTING

Since the accounting arm of my business was doing well with over a hundred clients in my books, I decided to focus my attention on business consulting, which had never been given the required strategy for growth.

Any qualified accountant can do accounting, but business consulting is a specialist skill and needs a personal touch. I had excellent knowledge and experience in both, and I knew it would benefit my clients.

My first strategy was to separate the business consulting from the accounting arm of my business. I registered it as Spearmans Consulting, which later became Spearmans UK.

My second strategy was to convert my accounting clients to business consulting clients by introducing these three business products to them:

1) Business Growth - strategies for improvement that ensures growth and expansion.

2) Succession Planning - to plan for a handover and prevent a business from collapsing when the owner is no longer there or passed away.

3) Detailed Tax planning – helping a business to save money through efficient tax planning.

My clients bought into this idea, and ninety-five percent of them became my business consulting clients, which was a hugely successful conversion rate. Therefore, this strategy was the best thing I could have done. This lasted for two to three years, and it was in the third year that I started to get about five percent per new client. My old partner and friend, Taggart, was instrumental in that.

SPEARMANS CONSULTING GOES INTERNATIONAL

Taggart relocated to Nigeria in 2011 to become a property magnate. It was definitely more profitable than the accounting business, so who could blame him for relocating? He was heavily involved in estate construction for both public and private sector clients.

Taggart referred any of his Nigerian clients who needed advice on their offshore financial and business operations to me, and I happily paid for those referrals. They were the perfect business consulting clients because they needed detailed tax planning to save them money.

Offshore was another name for tax havens, and I was able to advise them on that. It was an efficient and legal way to save money as a business, which was why many global corporations do it.

The process was simple. They register their business in a tax haven like Panama, Guernsey, or Switzerland. They open a business account in the tax haven, and all their payments are made into those offshore accounts. The only amount of tax they are required to pay is five hundred pounds, no matter how much they earn.

This is obviously a minimal amount, but some of these tax havens have a few strict terms and conditions to get more out of these companies. One is a requirement to have a local director and secretary and even a local address. Considering the tax savings they were making, these offshore companies gladly accepted these terms and conditions.

The number of Nigerian business consulting clients grew, and I had to travel to Nigeria every quarter to work there for a few days. In 2015, I set up SPEARMANS INSTITUTE OF ACCOUNTING in Nigeria and leased office premises in the Ikeja mainland area of Lagos.

These referrals from Taggart were like a repeat of our alliance years ago when we had just started collaborating in business, with him referring accounting clients to me and me reciprocating by referring my tax clients to him. He was always a pleasure to do business with and also a very good friend.

When I learnt Taggart was going through a difficult time because his estate construction clients in Nigeria delayed his payments for such long periods that the stress of it was affecting his health, I decided to propose another business partnership idea to him. I thought Taggart would be the perfect person to head the Spearmans business in Nigeria.

Sadly, I never got the chance to share my partnership idea with him because he passed away suddenly due to complications from a Covid-19 infection. The news of his death was like a 'punch in the chest' because he was my dear friend, and I still miss him. His death is such a huge loss.

FORMING NEW ALLIANCES

My business journey is full of alliances formed at every stage, and the main benefits are the cross-referrals that came out of it—my alliances with other accountants, restaurants, etc. Even when you do not form an alliance, networking opportunities are always valuable for accountants.

That is one of the great things about being an accountant because anyone who runs a business will always require your services. Clients will be drawn to you in any business premises where they know an accountant is present.

A good example was the large number of business referrals from customers who came to eat at Lekan's restaurant in Kilburn. The food suppliers to the restaurant saw our business sign in the window and simply walked into our office to sign up with us.

In every church I have attended as a regular member, I signed up many clients. All they needed to know was that there was an accountant in the church, and the church officials would request my services, and so did some fellow church members. I also offered my services to any business I deal with for cross-referral purposes.

Another opportunity for a business alliance came my way again when I shared an office with a Jewish Mortgage broker. It was a rewarding experience. He referred his mortgage clients to me for accounting services, and I referred my clients who needed a mortgage broker to him.

My business was doing wonderfully well and continued to grow. Although my goal of having some millionaire clients from the sports and entertainment industry on my books was never achieved, I was still a hugely successful businessman, accountant, and business consultant.

After a year of sharing the business premises with the mortgage broker, I moved into my office at Middlesex House, Edgware.

CELEBRATING TWENTY YEARS OF RUNNING MY OWN ACCOUNTING FIRM - (2000 - 2020).

Spearmans has continued to grow from strength to strength ever since and still operating as these three arms of business:

- Spearmans UK.

- Spearmans Consulting.

- Spearman Institute of Accounting.

In 2020, I organised a celebratory event in London to mark twenty years of running my own accounting firm. Although the business name has changed a few times, I remain the constant factor: me, Lance Kadiri, the accountant, and business consultant.

I am also proud to state that I am now a fellow of the accounting association, ACCA, which was awarded to me in 2001.

With my family at the celebration of my twentieth anniversary in business

The banner at the celebration of my twentieth anniversary in business -SPEARMANS UK

Web Images of a fictional character, Lance Spearman.

(Source: www.Facebook.com and www.chimureanga.co.za)

Chapter Twelve

My Message To The Next Generation

YOU HAVE READ my story in the preceding chapters. In this final chapter of my autobiography, I will share the life lessons that I have gathered in the course of my life's journey because I know many would find it beneficial.

THE FOUNDATION PERIOD

What I always tell my sons and the young generation is that they must start to work hard from year ten in secondary school. Focus on the compulsory subjects (English and Mathematics) and the other subjects that would get you into the university to study the degree of your choice.

Figure out the profession and career you want early on before your A Levels. Understandably, you may not know what you want to do now, so the best way to tackle this problem is to understand who you are and what you would be good at. These questions may help.

Example Questions:

- Are you an introvert or an extrovert?

- Are you detail-oriented?

- Do you like working with people as a team or prefer doing things alone?

- Do you like helping people?

- Do you enjoy public speaking and being in front of a camera?

- What are your interests?

- What are you passionate about?

If you find it challenging to arrive at the answers to any of the above questions, you should discuss it with your parents, relatives, or friends of the family. We know parents may try to influence your decision by imposing their career choices on you but do not rule it out because they know you better than anyone else. You should consider the advice because it may just be the right career for you, as in my case. Luckily for me, my father was subtle in his recommendation of the accounting profession and was able to get me interested in it. The decision to become an accountant became easier after that.

Another option is to find role models that interest you because you may want to emulate them. They could be celebrities or people in your family and friend circle. Look inwards and outwards. There are some professions that are difficult to find role models for, so you may have to search for one.

UNIVERSITY YEARS

As a university student, you must work even harder, especially in the first year, because this is the time most students become lazy with their studies and tend to lose focus. This can be attributed to the fact that it is their first taste of 'freedom' because many would be living on their own for the first time in their lives. As a result, they get carried away with the excitement of being totally independent from their parents and guardians. All they want to do is party every day and have fun.

Having good grades in the first and second year would improve your chances of attaining a first-class or second-class upper degree (2:1). This is the foundation and would make your final year of university less stressful. I wish someone had given me this advice in my first and second years because I would have partied less in my early years in university. I was on course to attain a second-class lower degree (2:2) until my internship when I was given a condition that only a 2:1 degree would guarantee me a job at the firm. Consequently, I had to work extra hard to attain my 2:1 degree, which could have been impossible.

EARLY CAREER BUILDING

I recommend an internship in a career that interests you because it would enable you to determine if it is the right career for you. It is a much-needed test. I was unsure if an accounting career was right for me until I did my internship at GAD Accountants.

Attend career days at university when companies come to do the 'MILK ROUND' because you will learn more about that career and also the opportunities available in those companies. These companies always pick the best students for internships, and this goes to buttress my point that working hard to get good grades in your first two years is imperative if you want to be selected.

THE ACCA QUALIFICATION

Once you get a job as an accountant, you must do all you can to attain this most sought-after ACCA qualification. Try to avoid any non-urgent 'distractions' if you can help it. You must have read my experience on this issue.

It has been said that the ACCA has been designed for only one in four people to pass the exam, which is about twenty-five percent. It is deliberately made difficult to keep the SCARCITY VALUE.

I recommend approaching the ACCA qualification as a master's degree because that is what it is - a post-graduate qualification.

I must point out that if you graduated from a top university like Oxford, Cambridge, or Harvard, it would probably be easier for you to pass the ACCA exam because you would be an 'A' star student anyway. That would give you an advantage; this group is in the minority. For others with lower qualifications like me, it becomes a 'Herculean challenge.'

POST - QUALIFICATION

There are two options available to you once you are qualified. You either go into practice or you work in the industry.

Working in Practice - this means working for an accounting firm. The goal here is to rise to the position of a partner. The best way to speed up your rise in a practice is to bring in big business. It has become achievable now for ethnic minorities to become named partners because there is less discrimination and racism these days. There are ethnic minorities named as partners in accounting firms today. That was impossible in the 90s when I was in practice.

Working in Industry: Working for a large corporation where you can rise to the finance director position. This remains one of the biggest challenges for accountants in the ethnic minority. In my accounting career that spans over thirty years, I have only met one black finance director at the helm of a corporation.

STARTING YOUR OWN FIRM

Do not go it alone at the beginning of your business career–partner with another accountant who has a different accounting specialisation. Then you need a marketer or an accountant who can market and network as a bonus. Who's better to market accounting products than an accountant who understands the products and services?

Learn from my mistakes narrated in this book. At Lance. Lincoln & Co, Lekan was the marketer who helped to generate business for the firm. At Lance/Taggart/West

we had Deji West doing the marketing. I recommend starting as a partnership because two heads are better than one, increasing your chances of success.

MY MESSAGE TO BLACK ACCOUNTANTS WORLDWIDE

There are more black accounting firms today than we had in the 90s. Why can't we have a global accounting firm of black accountants with over twenty partners like KPMG, ANDERSON CONSULTING, OR DELOITTE?

It could be achieved through a merger, which was what these firms did.

That was my vision for our partnership, Lance, Taggart, West & Co, but it never happened. I hope that in the not-too-distant future, the next generation will achieve that. I shall continue to hope and pray it happens someday.

ABOUT THE
BLACK BEAN COUNTER

This book will not be complete without explaining what the phrase 'Bean counter' means and why I call myself the Black Bean Counter. The below statements define it perfectly.

Bean Counter Meaning

"Definition: An accountant or other person who controls the budget down to the smallest amounts of money or other aspects of account keeping. More generally, someone who deals with numbers."

Origin of Bean Counter

"The first use of this expression with the current meaning was in the early 1900s. The idea behind the expression is that beans are so small that counting them individually is a waste of time. Only someone overly concerned with minute details would do that".

(Source: https://writingexplained.org/idiom-dictionary/bean-counter**)**

Being a black accountant makes me a Black Bean Counter. This is my story, and I hope you enjoyed it.

The Black Bean Counter in 2023.